Assault on Marriage

A Christian's Response

Thomas D. Logie

Order this book online at www.trafford.com
or email orders@trafford.com

Most Trafford titles are also available at major online book retailers.

Printed in the United States of America.

ISBN: 978-1-4669-6639-0 (sc)
ISBN: 978-1-4669-6638-3 (e)

Trafford rev. 11/08/2012

North America & international
toll-free: 1 888 232 4444 (USA & Canada)
phone: 250 383 6864 • fax: 812 355 4082

Foreword

In the November 12, 2012 edition of *Fortune* magazine, Adam Lashinsky and Katie Benner wrote a provocative article entitled "The Odd Couple" about a new marriage between two wealthy financiers, Alphonse Fletcher, Jr. and Ellen Pao. Married in 2007, both husband and wife find themselves in conflicts at work and under financial pressure. While their assets and potential debts are much larger than the average person, the article reveals pressures that seem typical of their generation. Past relationships, litigation, geographical separation and enormous workweeks are similar to the troubles so many other marriages face in the financial world. Although most people do not face these particular troubles, the ones they do face are more similar than different. The article concludes that the marriage partners' troubles seem to have driven them together for the time being.

If indeed they stay together through thick and thin, Mr. Fletcher and Ms. Pao will have come upon something more precious than any amount of money and other assets that they are able to garner and retain: an enduring marriage. As Solomon said long ago, *"Better is a little with the fear of the Lord than great treasure and trouble with it. Better is a dinner of herbs where love is than a stalled ox and hatred with it."* Proverbs 15:16-17. In that day a stalled ox represented wealth and capital; if the ox were female, the asset could readily multiply over time. But fear of God and marital love are both better. *"Better is a little with righteousness than great revenues without right ... How much better it is to get wisdom than gold! To get understanding to be chosen rather than silver."* Proverbs 16:8, 16. An enduring, loving marriage is precious and in the modern era increasingly rare. I would pray that this couple and millions more will find and enjoy these riches. But even with the riches of precious marriage, people need to remember that the most secure riches are those with God in heaven (Matthew 6:19-33).

The greatest love remains the love of Jesus Christ for sinners shown at the Cross where He gave His life a ransom for many. The end result expressed in Revelation 21-22 is the intimacy between Jesus Christ and His Bride, the Church. Ephesians 5:22-33 also hints at this. On earth the most intimate love is between husband and wife. And then there are other forms of love and friendship, such as family love and close bonds between best friends. But the greatest love of all, which can make everlasting bonds of lesser forms of love, is the love of the entire Trinity expressed and revealed in the love, death and resurrection of Jesus Christ.

Introduction to Part One

Most of this book will be written from a distinctly Biblical and Christian perspective, because I believe that Biblical Christianity is the way that God offers the human race back from the brink of disaster. At the outset, we should note that God has given marriage not only to the Church but to the entire human race as one of the major foundation corners of civilization itself. Innumerable observers from ancient and modern societies have noted that marriage has a stabilizing effect on men which is of great benefit to the entire human race. To take but one example from the world of sports, a loving wife was Josh Hamilton's human rescue line from a life of debilitating drugs to the recovery of his vocation as a baseball player. Josh Hamilton himself would tell you that Jesus Christ had everything to do with his recovery and that his wife was one of the major people He used to bring this about. But even apart from Christianity and Judaism and before either Christianity or Judaism existed in organized form, marriage has been a universal necessity of any civilization or society, from jungle tribes to modern cities. The original marriage of Adam and Eve even predates the fall of Satan and the subsequent contamination of the human race by sin. Even Adam before his first sin needed a female wife as a companion. So when I seek to defend marriage, I am defending part of the foundation of civilization itself, not only a part of the foundation of the Christian church.

One of the major problems facing the Christian church at large is the high divorce rate both in society as a whole and among those couples who attend church. How should church leaders advise their members, especially young adults, on how to choose a marriage partner? There is no one Biblical text or even any combination of texts that addresses that question directly. One reason for this is that marriage is intended for most people of marriageable age in the community, not just within a church. Human beings have tried various methods. Jacob was smitten with Rachel from the minute he saw her and worked 7 years to marry her. For now we will ignore Laban's mischief and the cooperation of both Leah and Rachel in it. In some societies marriages are arranged by parents with the actual mates having little to say about who they marry. This was true in most European royal families. This pattern often holds true even today in Pakistan and India and among polygamous societies. I cannot imagine any young woman of good sense consenting to marry a man already married to another and facing a lifetime prospect of having to share her husband with one or more entrenched wives.

If parents are arranging marriages, their motives have varied. Some have honestly tried to make good choices either from knowing their child's potential partners or at least knowing their family histories and making educated guesses from that knowledge. Others have married off their children for wealth, prestige or power. Others still have hired matchmakers from their community. This often was done among Eastern European Jews before World War 2. In Romania, there was for centuries a custom of marriage fairs at which young men and young women would pair off. This is actually similar to the method used in Israel when the tribe of Benjamin needed to be repopulated. Benjamin had almost been wiped out when the tribe resisted divine justice against Gibeah (see Judges 19-20). Unmarried women from a town that had not participated in destroying Benjamin for its defense of Gibeah's sin were brought to Benjamin's male survivors, who chose wives for themselves.

In America and the West, we believe that children coming of age have the right to decide for themselves whom to marry and whether to marry at all. This system seems to have worked reasonably well until the 1960s, although there was deterioration before that. The Scriptures do set certain limits in the choice of marriage partners. Incest was forbidden once there was a sufficient world population where the prohibition would be practical. (Obviously, this could not be done in the generation of Cain and Abel when only sisters would have been available as wives for them. There would have been similar problems in the early generations after Noah. Thus Abram married his half-sister Sarai (Genesis 20:12) without condemnation, and even Lot's daughters did not receive the condemnation that they would receive today. They had some honest basis after seeing an entire region burnt to ashes to believe that once again they were among the last survivors and that their father was the only person available to make them pregnant. They neglected to pray and proceeded only on their own observation, which was wrong. Nonetheless God did not at that time condemn their acts of seducing their father as we would condemn similar conduct today, as the Austrian father who committed incest with his daughter a few years ago was condemned severely and justly. This is an instance in which the Law of Moses, given long after Lot's days, *"[has made] sin exceedingly sinful."* Romans 7:13).

For believers, the most fundamental limitation on our liberty to marry is that we must marry a fellow believer. As Paul wrote of a widow, she was *"free to marry whom she will, only in the Lord."* 1 Corinthians 7:39. At any stage of life, a marriage between a believer and an umbeliever has a fault line running through it that can rupture at any time with devastating effect. This does not always happen but it does frequently. For one Old Testament example, consider the disastrous effects of Samson's relationship with Delilah, resulting in Samson's blindness and enslavement. Solomon's original marriage with an Egyptian princess for political reasons was less than a resounding success. As Solomon later ignored her in favor of his 700 wives and 300 concubines, Egypt turned cool to Israel and harbored Jeroboam, who had rebelled against Solomon and fled there. After Solomon's death Jeroboam divided the entire kingdom. So Solomon's political marriage eventually became a source of disaster after his death.

If both marriage partners are indeed believers, as both of them grow closer to Jesus Christ they will also grow closer to each other. Young people marrying for the first time must realize that they cannot have a perfect mate or be a perfect mate themselves. If one studies Proverbs, one will find recurring patterns for consideration in a mate. I would recommend strongly that both parties study Proverbs separately and ideally together before they marry and set up their household. Taking one chapter per day, this should take a month. A hot temper and laziness are traits that cause special trouble in marriage. Proverbs 31 is a blueprint for a superb wife, but one can hardly expect a young person with little experience to have attained this degree of sanctification already. Likewise it is rare for a young man to be ready to serve as a deacon or pastor as described in 1 Timothy 3 and Titus 1 without already having experience in family life.

In Part One of this book I will create a fictional narrative to try to frame various issues in the formation of marriage and the selection of a mate. I am not attempting to write a good novel and will give only the barest attention to the setting and other incidental details that would concern a writer of fiction for its own sake. My purpose is to frame Scriptural and practical issues for discussion and debate and to bring Holy Scripture into focus. When I use the term "football" in this narrative, I am using it in the English sense. Americans would call the game soccer. "Manchester Fusion" is a fictional football side; in 2012 the two strongest English teams in the Premier League were Manchester City and Manchester United. Use your imagination and take your pick. So far as I know, the Penzeance Privateers are entirely fictional. Part Two will be an exposition of 1 Corinthians 7, one of the most neglected Scriptures in the Christian church today. The remaining portion will deal with a comparison and contrast between marriage on earth and life in heaven.

Part 1

Chapter 1

Mrs. Kerr went to her office of the National Health Service in St. Andrews, Scotland to review her breast cancer screening results. Still pretty in her middle 50s, she had been feeling tired but without other obvious symptoms. Since there was no apparent emergency, it had taken almost 2 months to arrange a routine appointment, which had been combined with a mammogram. Her tests had been run over 2 weeks ago and now she was learning her results. The doctor tried his best to conceal her concern, but there is no way to buffer a diagnosis of metastasized breast cancer spread to the bone and probably to the liver. Mrs. Kerr called her husband at his office. He was the owner in charge of a small but prosperous supply company which ran food and other supplies to the drilling platforms in the North Sea. Mr. Kerr was a solid executive and administrator who without bombast left no doubt who was in charge. He arrived from his office a few minutes later and joined the his wife and the NHS doctor in conference. However, the extent that the cancer had spread left little hope of recovery. The doctor advised that Mrs. Kerr probably had about 6 months to live. She and her husband hugged each other; then Mrs. Kerr was able to compose herself sufficiently to drive her car home. Both of them were in shock.

Their daughter Julie was 21 years old and finishing her studies at the university. She was slender, red-head and nearly five feet eight inches. Julie had been a dutiful and diligent student with a cheerful disposition. Her grades were quite good. Underneath she had a share of her father's determination, but this was easy to miss unless one watched her closely for an extended period of time. She was studying biology because she was good at it and enjoyed it, but she did not have a definite plan of how she would use her knowledge and her degree once she had obtained it. She too was shocked at the diagnosis and cried with her mother. But there was nothing for Julie to do but to continue her studies. At this stage her mother did not require special care, so Julie continued her studies and home life still had a semblance of normalcy. Julie did scale back her social activities to make sure that she spent time with her mother while she could.

Mr. Kerr tried to scale back his duties at work when possible in order to spend more time with his ailing wife. A computer could be set up at home and files could be shared between the two computers. But this worked only so far. In some cases Mr. Kerr's personal touch was needed to keep the business in balance. As winter turned into early spring Mrs. Kerr declined sharply and the strain increased on both Mr. Kerr and her daughter. Mr. Kerr tried to handle only essential tasks and Julie basically limited herself to her classes and other educational assignments. Mrs. Kerr declined any extreme treatment and passed away on April 1.

Julie with her normally cheerful disposition began to bounce back soon after her mother's funeral, but Mr. Kerr had more trouble adjusting to singleness after 30 years of marriage. He began to have a couple of drinks after dinner at home, which he had not done before. Mr. Kerr did not become completely intoxicated, but Julie was still concerned about his behavior. Mr. Kerr brushed her off and try to bury himself in his work. Partly this was to make up neglected work during Mrs. Kerr's last weeks of life and partly to numb his grief. Mr. Kerr had no major social interests outside his work and few friends besides his daughter. His business colleagues likewise concentrated on company business. With Julie recovering faster than her father, their moods diverged and each became less comfortable with the other. Mr. Kerr wondered if Julie was disrespectful to her mother when she was cheerful, and Julie worried that her father was sinking into gloom and tried ways to get Mr. Kerr to enjoy something outside his work, without much success. Julie had largely taken over the cooking as her mother declined, but then she had to go to school and her father to work.

Naturally, Mr. Kerr wondered about Julie's plans after graduation that spring. They discussed teaching, graduate study or specialized training in medicine or an allied field. Julie was unsure and pointed out that the job market was not robust. Julie's field of study was not suited for work with her father's firm and neither raised that possibility. Julie had no inclination to train as her father's successor and her father did not see the makings of a business executive in her.

Julie and her mother and father had briefly discussed the subject of marriage before Mrs. Kerr had died. Julie said simply that she did not know any man that interested her and that she was not in a hurry. Her parents advised her that she should consider the advantages of wealth in a marriage partner. Her father offered to make discreet inquiry to try to locate a suitable man who would be a suitable match in their estimation. She would live in material comfort without the typical worries of the middle class. Julie would have more freedom to enjoy life. It might even happen that her future husband would help with Mr. Kerr's business. Like the fictional family in *Titanic*, the Kerrs was interested in carrying and increasing the family fortune and status through marriage, much as royal families for centuries have married off daughters for reason of diplomacy. Julie demurred at this. She wanted to marry for love rather than money and to make her own choice. The scions of wealthy families of whom Julie knew seemed soft and weak because they had been given so many privileges so easily. That did not suit Julie; she wanted a man who would bear responsibility personally. In this respect her father's example as the CEO of both his company and his family rubbed off, although neither of them discussed this aspect of the subject.

Julie was not specific about how she viewed or defined love and her parents did not make love a first priority because they believed that love or at least mutual respect would develop after the marriage. They viewed common interests, upbringing, family backgrounds and class status (unless Julie were able to "marry up", which in her parents' eyes would be better yet) as more solid foundations for marriage than love, at least considered as romance. They pointed out the fact that money issues play a major role in many divorces. Julie's approach was more like a person who learns by specific example instead of general precept. She expected to recognize love when she saw it. While this is the experience of some people, this approach does not lend itself well to prior planning or discussion as the parents desired. Religion did not enter into the discussions at all.

But Julie had no immediate ideas of marriage in any case while she was still completing her undergraduate studies, so these discussions had no urgency. She was not yet ready to give focused consideration to marriage or even to whether she would or would not marry at all in the foreseeable future. There was a potential clash of ideas about how to assess a potential husband for Julie but this issue remained in the background while Mrs. Kerr was alive and for about a month after Mrs. Kerr's death and funeral. But by then Julie desired to resume some student social life. With that, the potential for being attracted to a young man reopened.

QUESTIONS FOR REFLECTION & DISCUSSION

1. What help can or should a pastor and other church members offer when a person who regularly attends church is given a terminal diagnosis?
2. In the story, the father and daughter made adjustments but maintained most of their regular activities. Was this appropriate?
3. A month after her mother's death, was it appropriate for her daughter to start to resume some social life? Some people believe that a widow or widower should not marry for some specified time after the death of the spouse. Is some waiting period usually wise to let the survivor settle down? Is there any support in the Scriptures for a specified waiting period mandatory for everyone?

4. There will be much more discussion later on, but to what extent should financial considerations determine when a person should marry? How much difference does age make?
5. What is your reaction to Mr. Kerr taking two drinks between dinner and bedtime where he had not done this before? How would you compare this to the taking of a sedative or an anti-anxiety prescription? Was the daughter's concern justified?

Part 1

Chapter 2

About two years before Mrs. Kerr's death, Alexander ("Sandy") Thomas was playing goalie for Hartlepool, a football team in the lower half of League One, two tiers below England's Premier League. Sandy's roots were in Scotland, and it was convenient that Sandy was playing in a city only 50 miles or so from the traditional Scottish border. Unlike many footballers, Sandy read extensively, stayed away from the nightlife, alcohol and drugs and took good care of his body. Sandy had gained notoriety several years earlier at age 19 as the goalkeeper for the level 12 side that had shocked the mighty Manchester Fusion in the third round of the FA Cup. He had risen to League One, but his career was now stalled with no immediate prospects of advancement. In fact, Sandy was being pressed for his starting position by a younger, taller goalkeeper with several inches of additional arm reach. Sandy positioned himself aggressively to cut down shooting angles and was a strong leader. He was playing well, although he was short in both height and reach compared to most goalkeepers. But at 25 Sandy was not able to attract attention from any teams in either the Premier League or the Championship League, and he wondered whether he would be benched in favor of his younger colleague to get him experience.

Sandy's suspicions were increased when he was directed to represent the club at a half-day clinic for young teen players outside the city. This would entail an absence from practice. Sandy concealed his disappointment and dutifully went to the clinic, where he was in charge of teaching the goalkeepers. Sandy completed his three hours at the clinic and prepared to return to his well-worn car when an older gentleman approached and introduced himself. "I'm Donald Johnstone," he said. "What's your name?"

"I'm Sandy Thomas. I play goal for Hartlepool and hope to move higher." In his mind, Sandy wondered whether this was the famous . . .

"I have never met you, but you might know of me from my earlier days at Glasgow Rangers when they were at the top of the Scottish Premier League. I must compliment you on how you ran your part of the clinic."

"Thank you," Sandy said. "But why were you watching a small clinic like this?"

"I love football and I have a grandson who was with the forwards. He had a cousin with him. I looked at the goalkeepers and noticed that you made a natural connection with the lads.

That's a gift from God and is not something that anyone can teach. You had them well organized and I really think that most of them learned something to improve them. I have been in football for over 50 years and God has so far kept my eyes keen. You have a gift for teaching."

Sandy had been asked to teach Sunday School and youth meetings occasionally and knew that others agreed that he had a gift for teaching. But he said to Mr. Johnstone, "Like any athlete I want to improve and move up. I would hope to get a shot in the Premier League or at least in the Championship. What's holding me back?"

Mr. Johnstone replied, "Lad, God did not make you to be a world-class goalkeeper. If He had intended that, He would have given you more height and longer arms. Look at someone like Brad Friedel, the American who plays for Tottenham. Peter Cech of Chelsea is thinner than Friedel but still very tall and long. Joe Hart of Manchester City is similar. With tall strikers like Peter Crouch and Dirk Kuyt, the day of the short, quick, compact goalkeeper—and you are short by modern standards—is over. You play well, but your physical limits stop you from further progress as a player. You need to become a coach. When your contract has run, come see me in Glasgow and I will help you get started."

Sandy said, "Thank you for your compliments. But I desire to serve God as much as possible when my career is over, not just teach football."

Mr. Johnstone surprised Sandy by saying, "So much the better. You can do both. Put together the clinics and training and have a Bible study during a break or at the end of the sessions when the lads are tired enough to settle down and listen. You can minister to both body and soul."

"Are you a believer in Jesus Christ?" Sandy asked.

"Yes," replied Mr. Johnstone. "I had heard about a goalkeeper in Hartlepool that had a reputation of being a man of faith, and now I realize that you are the one. Kaka has a reputation of being devout, and a pioneer footballer in the United States, Kyle Rote, Jr., was outspoken in his advocacy of the Christian faith. So you have some company despite football's rough reputation established by people like the late Georgie Best and Wayne Rooney in the present day. The time when minds are most open to the Christian faith is when lads are young before they get caught up in the temptations of life in sports. From seeing you teach today, I am convinced that this is your calling and want to help you get started when your contract is up."

"Then I should come to see you in early May when our league schedule is finished?"

"Yes, do come. I will make contacts in the meantime and help with seed money." So they set a specific appointment about a month away after the season and the contract were over, and Sandy found that Mr. Johnstone was better than his word. Over the next two years Sandy worked diligently to make his instruction available at prices that many players could afford, and the proceeds together with occasional gifts and supplements were sufficient to provide for Sandy's basic needs. Sandy also began to speak to university and teenage groups as an evangelist and teacher of Christianity in his spare time.

QUESTIONS FOR REFLECTION & DISCUSSION:

1. Have you have had a surprise, life-changing encounter? Do you believe that God can and does arrange the unexpected?
2. Mr. Thomas' progress as a goalkeeper was blocked by factors which he could not control. (Matthew 6:27) Have you found that God may close one door to direct you to another? (Consider Acts 16:6-10)
3. Football in England has many rough characters, like sports teams in many countries. In other fields, Christians may also mix with many whose lives are far from godly. For example, how would you react as a teacher or banker if you learned that your colleague or supervisor was a drug seller or stripper after hours? Clearly, you can't join them, but how do you react apart from refusing to take part in such activities (consider 1 Peter 4:1-7)?
4. To what extent do you consider the ability to teach to be gift of God instead of something that can be learned by instruction and practice?

Part 1

Chapter 3

The students filed into the large lecture hall, which was about half full. Julie attended the lecture with some friends for lack of something more interesting that night. The friends expected to ridicule the speaker and maybe even heckle him. The speaker was Alexander Thomas, a retired footballer, age 27, who had one moment of fame, when his Level 12 side shocked Manchester Fusion in the third round of the FA Cup. His moment of football fame was far from his mind as he was being introduced to the student and faculty audience. Most of the students didn't care about his football background. His subject of Creation was sure to draw ridicule from some. He prayed under his breath as the host gestured him to the podium. Still youthful and having avoided serious injury from his football, he strode to the platform and started as follows:

Good evening and thank you so much for coming for coming on a rainy night like this. My subject is the Christian view of Creation, which cannot be reconciled with the scientific orthodoxy of neo-Darwinian random evolution. Darwin's theory as carried forward into modern times requires that life has not only evolved from species to species but has done so in random fashion, with no guiding intelligence of any kind. This is a necessary part of Darwinism because this is the only way that men and women can be their own gods. As soon as one opens the door to any form of intelligence guiding an evolutionary process, one then is confronted with the question of how we as intelligent beings must relate to that intelligence. This is precisely what modern humanity wants to escape. So for the sake even of intellectual honesty it is vital to focus on the issue of randomness in nature.

Let's start with dogs. So far nobody has reported the offspring of two dogs becoming something radically different from a dog. Indeed Darwin's original theory posits glacially slow change, not anything sudden. Suggestions of sudden mutations have been made later because of gaps in Darwin's theory, but the mutation suggestions are not borne out either by the evidence. We observe new breeds and cross-breeds arising, such as the "Goldendoodle." In the plant world there is constant genetic experimentation with wheat, corn and rice. But these are not random—quite the contrary. These adaptations are guided by men and women utilizing selective breeding and gene splicing. One can debate the degree of intelligence in the execution of these techniques to favor desired characteristics and to suppress others, but we cannot dispute that there is some intelligence guiding the changes. (*A few chuckles)* These instances of micro-evolution within species which we all know exist are not random and in fact are evidence against the idea that the evolution that does exist is in fact random instead of directed.

Darwin himself knew nothing about genetics when he published *Origin of Species* in 1859. With the equipment and knowledge base of his time he could examine structure but knew nothing of the genetic code. While Mendel was working on plant genetics, it was to be approximately a century before Crick and Watson were able to discover the double helix. While I will be criticizing Darwin's theory in the light of additional 150-plus years of scientific knowledge, I will pay tribute to his intellect and to his painstaking observations. He himself proposed a test for his own theory in his book, "*If it could be demonstrated that any complex organ existed, which could not possibly have been formed by numerous, successive, slight modifications, my theory [of evolution] would absolutely break down. But I can find out no such case.*" From a scientific standpoint, it is generally accepted that any theory that requires two or more structures to evolve simultaneously is too improbable under the laws of mathematics to be accepted.

A scientific debate of Intelligent Design v. Random Evolution rages to this moment within science despite the efforts of random evolution defenders to ridicule Intelligent Design advocates as stupid or unscientific. If you will read James Behe or Phillip Johnson with any kind of open mind you will have to conclude that they are intelligent writers with a large fund of scientific knowledge. James Behe believes that the microscopic paramecium is already too complex to have been the product of random evolution because of the need for five distinct structures for even a single-celled form of life to survive and reproduce. And these reproduce by cell division rather than by sexual reproduction as more complex form of life do. In more complex cases there is a requirement for a simultaneous matched pair of a series of organs and structures at the same location that will enable the exchange between male and female that will form new life. Gradual evolution seems impossible under Darwin's own test because 80% or 90% compliance with the requirements would still leave a sterile or even fatal adaptation with no further possibility of advancement.

Whitaker Chambers, the American ex-Communist, was dissuaded from Communism when as a father he could not believe that the human eye could have evolved randomly. This became a matter of historical importance when his testimony led to the exposure of Alger Hiss as a Communist mole in the United States government and increased British vigilance to the point that Kim Philby fled to the Soviet Union. Sometime great consequences flow from small moments.

I know that Paley raised the issue of the complexity of the eye more than a century before Chambers. Evolutionists try to answer this with a scenario under which the most photo-sensitive path could have been followed as the eye evolved. But this overlooks that humanity does not have the most sensitive eye possible in nature. Many animals have keener eyesight and a keener senses of smell and hearing than do human beings. If drug dealers had to cope only with the human nose, their life would be so easy. But when a trained dog is brought into the scene, then the probability of detection rises dramatically. So in the animal world we are not dealing with one common sense of smell, hearing or sight, but many unique senses that are attuned to the needs of survival long enough to reproduce after its own kind of each organism. Bats have radar, but humans do not as a sense of the human body. We do not fully understand the senses of marine mammals either. But we do know that diverse packages of senses that fit the brains and the body structure of each type of life do exist. I submit that this is not evidence of random evolution but of intelligent creation.

We certainly observe micro-evolution within species, such as changes in different breeds of dogs. A few closely related species can interbreed, but the offspring is normally sterile, such as a mule. Some mammals beside human beings can learn limited new behaviors, but this does not make them a new species. But the new varieties we do see are not random but designed, whether hybrid grains or cross-bred dogs. And evolution has no explanation for why aging and death is universal. A universal phenomenon is not evidence of randomness but of intelligent control. The Bible may be mocked today, but it does have a coherent explanation of why living creatures on earth all die. The entire Creation is in bondage to death because of sin. [Romans 8:18-23]

Switching from scientific observation to historical observation, a belief in macro-evolution undermines a sense of right and wrong. Evolutionary logic applied to human beings means that the strong should enslave or even kill the weak. That sounds like the Mongols or the Dark Ages, doesn't it? Adolf Hitler was a rigorous evolutionist. For most of his life he claimed that the Germans were the fittest race to rule the world and that the Jews were sub-human and the Slavic peoples were next to the bottom. Therefore, the German Nazis sought world rule by any means within their reach without regard to any moral standards at all. Their ideology encouraged murder, sexual predation, stealing, lying and any conduct that they thought would work. This is like the actions of a new male tiger or lion in a territory who will try to kill the existing cubs in order to force the mother to mate with him. We get a faint human echo in the abusive conduct of some step-parents who want their step-children out of their way to make way for either themselves or their future children.

Near the end of his life, Hitler came to believe that the Russians were stronger in an evolutionary sense and therefore thought that the German people should be ground into the dust. The methods of the Russian secret police were similar to those of the Nazis. The massacre of Katyn Woods is one example. Most evolutionists do not take their conduct nearly this far, but nevertheless it is logically true that believers in random evolution have no room for the sacred. For them there is no concept of holiness or righteousness. There is a strong correlation between belief in random evolution and the belief in a master race or a dictatorial ruling elite. If the rule of the strongest is a biological imperative, where is the room for freedom for all?

In Stalinist Russia the influence of evolution for a time led to Lysenko's notion that characteristics acquired by environmental influence could be transmitted genetically in plants. Stalin extended Lysenko's idea to the belief that the new "Socialist man" could be made superior by environmental training as opposed to the Nazi notion of genetic superiority. Both of these opposing ideas are thoroughly and aggressively atheistic but are opposite in the vaunted source of their supposed superiority. In both cases the overgrown senses of pride and superiority led to frightful injustices by these dictators and their minions against the people.

Another reaction to evolution is maximized pleasure-seeking and selfishness as opposed to self-aggrandizement as a member of a ruling class. If we have no higher purpose than ourselves, this is a natural reaction. As the Apostle Paul in 1 Corinthians

15:32 quoted a Latin poet, *"Let us eat and drink, for tomorrow we die."* You observe this in the camaraderie shown in beer commercials. This is very far from what Paul believed, but the apostle recognized this sentiment as the logical conclusion of the belief that there is no resurrection from the dead. I cannot think of anyone who believes in random evolution, as distinguished from some believers in theistic evolution theories of bygone times, who also believes in the resurrection of the dead. A logical evolutionist will seek to enjoy the ride through life as long as it may last. A Christian like the Apostle Paul will view the herd of humanity as like lemmings speeding frantically to their own destruction; unlike the lemmings, that destruction will continue after physical death. For Paul, one of the greatest motives to do right was the general resurrection of the dead and the Last Judgment. Such motivation is logically impossible for someone who believes in random evolution and thus in bodily death as the termination of all existence.

I submit that our brains and our eyes and ears tell us that the universe is not the product of a random process because of the recurring order that we observe not only in bodily structure of both plants and animals but also in DNA and RNA. We know that computer programs do not leap into action from mere numbers without human intervention, so it is absurd to believe that DNA and RNA developed randomly. Moreover, we know that dissimilar organisms depend on one another. Humans need favorable organisms in their digestive tract; that is why yogurt is good for us. Such organisms need human beings as hosts also. Bears need both fish and honeybees for their diet. Large mammals need tree leaves and grass as well as water, which by itself could not evolve. Neither could oxygen nor carbon dioxide evolve, because they do not themselves have life. On earth the force of gravity is just the right strength—how does the evolutionist explain that?

I submit likewise that our consciences, not to mention the Bible, tell us that the ethical consequences of belief in random evolution are unacceptable. History confirms the testimony of conscience.

So if random evolution is wrong scientifically and ethically, where does that take us? Proving that our environment is designed rather than random from scientific reasoning does not of itself give us any proof of how or by whom our environment—and we ourselves—have been designed. Scientific argument can take us no farther.

This is where the Bible gives answers where science cannot because of our human limitations. The Bible tells us that indeed we have eternal purpose as living companions of God Himself. The Father, Son and Spirit all cooperated to make us in His image—not in the image of the animal kingdom—to love Him forever and to be loved by Him. That original image of God was mutilated by sin, but Jesus Christ as the Son of God in human flesh came to earth, was crucified and rose from the dead to set in motion a chain of events still in progress that is restoring the image of God in somewhat the same way as our archeologists would restore an ancient piece of art which has been painted over or ravaged by time and weather. This is still in progress. We are all broken beyond repair by human means. That is part of what death means and signifies. But the power of God through Jesus Christ does heal, restore and undo all—not part but all—of the destruction by sin and Satan. He offers that grace to each of you tonight. He does not require you to earn anything, but only to surrender and stop fighting

Him, insulting Him and running from Him. That means that you admit not only specific sins but your sinful human nature and believe that as God Jesus will deliver you from the natural and just consequences of your sin. He has already paid the price on the Cross—now your responsibility is true faith and genuine repentance so that the blood-price may be applied to your account.

Q1: Did I understand you to argue that because of the symbiosis between parasite and host and the relationship between predator and prey mean that the world is one large complex system that could not reasonably have come together by evolution?

Yes. You expanded from my argument concerning the complexity of a single organism with excellent insight. You could mix that in with an environment that favors life.

Q2: What do you say about the human fetus going through various stages that appear to be evolutionary?

The environment for a baby inside the mother's womb is very different from that after birth. Darkness and amniotic fluid are key features prior to birth. Therefore it is sound engineering for a pre-born child to have structures suitable for a liquid environment, similar to gills in fish. But certainly there is no direct light for eyes to see in the womb, so their initial development of the eye is not a response to the initial environment. If eyes in theory could have developed after birth in response to light, are we not back to the Lysenko problem where he claimed that plants could develop genetic traits reflecting changes after initial conception or birth? One would have to face the difficulty that the newborn child can see in light and dark immediately even though there was no prior environmental stimulus of that type. The growth of an infant in the womb must be designed because there is no exposure to our present environment—for example, to the atmosphere with free oxygen and other gases—prior to birth.

I might summarize this point this way. At conception for a human being or other large animal, there is the darkness of the womb rather than the light of day. Therefore, the development of the eye and of the structures such as the optic nerve and the parts of the brain necessary to process and interpret images seen by the eye cannot be a response to an environment that exists at conception. It is in response to a future environment unknown to the newly forming life. But that environment is known to the Creator, Whom the Bible identifies as the triune God: Father, Son and Holy Spirit. The preparation within the womb for a vastly different environment after birth is evidence of forethought and therefore of design and likewise speaks against random evolution.

Q3. Why are the majority of scientists evolutionists? Isn't it because of the evidence they see?

No. We cannot replicate in experiments what a theoretical earth and atmosphere looked like before life was present, and therefore we have no basis for an experiment using the scientific method. While God was building the earth—and evolutionists will admit that they have to assume an environment where life was possible—He was putting into place the elements and their bonding properties for compounds that support life. Ideologically, most scientists eliminate divine Creation and from that initial presumption imagine various evolutionary hypotheses. Their convictions cannot be based on evidence that does not exist.

Instead, they are following what they have been taught in the face of mounting evidence to the contrary. And one of the main reasons why this is so is because most scientists want to avoid the issues that present themselves as soon as we admit that there is a Creator. It makes us feel powerless. We want to feel powerful, but there are limits. If we thought that we could fly like birds without an airplane or a helicopter and actually tried it, we would discover our error with drastic consequences so quickly that we would not have time to learn from it or attempt to evolve to overcome it. Even on grounds of realism, we have to admit to an orderly Creation and therefore to a Creator. As David wrote in Psalm 19:1, *"The heavens declare the glory of God, and the firmament shows His handiwork."*

Q4. What is your opinion about whether Scotland should be an independent nation again?

Scotland has a historical heritage that should not be forgotten. Wallace and Robert the Bruce fought to defend independence in a day when English kings were tyrannical more often than not. John Knox and the Covenanters both stood for the truth that a King or Queen is a sinner like any other person and must be subject to the Law of God like all others. They stood for the right of the individual to worship God according to conscience regardless of the faith of the Crown. James and Robert Haldane pioneered in church planting and Bible exposition. Imagine what kind of society we would have if we had a combination of modern technology and the spiritual fervor for Jesus Christ that existed under leaders like that. Imagine if Scottish families still stood together and divorce were rare, with the blessings of modern technology. You wouldn't be near heaven but you might feel like it. It is far more important for Scotland to be spiritually subject to Jesus Christ than to be either within Great Britain or independent as a Scottish Republic.

Q5. What about other religions with different explanations of Creation?

One would have to look one by one to see how much sense the varying explanations of Creation make. However, Christianity has one unique element that stamps it as true—a Teacher that submitted to an unjust death on a cruel Roman Cross and then rose from the dead and showed Himself to hundreds of witnesses. He also left behind three people whom He brought back from the dead—Lazarus, a young man who was the sole support of his widowed mother and a younger girl about 12 years old at the time. No doctor, Luke included, has even come close to healing as many people from as many illnesses and injuries as did Jesus Christ. I would agree to a degree with anyone who says that the universe and everything in it has been designed, but only Jesus Christ has demonstrated on earth the power to control Creation and of His own power to reverse death itself.

Q. Why are Christianity and Islam so antagonistic to one another?

The most fundamental difference is that Christianity is a faith where the sacrificial love of the Son of God is at the very core. Islam agrees that Jesus Christ was virgin-born and that He was sinless, but denies that Jesus Christ was actually crucified because such a death for Him violates the Islamic sense of justice. But Jesus Christ agreed to take the sins of His people upon Himself in order to satisfy divine justice on our behalf (1 Peter 2:24).

Like most faiths other than Biblical Christianity, Islam believes that people earn salvation from God by good works. Some of the particular good works of Islam, such as dying in battle in a holy war, which we also find in Japanese Shinto, may differ from the good works commended by other religions, but the essential structure of an earned salvation remains. In contrast, Christianity as taught in the Bible teaches that Jesus Christ paid the entire price of the salvation of all who will ever be saved. We can and should obey Him and do good works in gratitude for what He has done, but we never contribute anything to our salvation.

Christianity and Islam agree that Abraham is one of the pivotal figures in human history, but once again they take opposite tacks from there. Islam quite conventionally claims that the oldest son is the heir of the promises to Abraham. Christians agree that Ishmael is the progenitor of the Arab peoples and that Abraham's prayer for Ishmael was heard and has been answered by God. Ishmael's Arab descendents have multiplied and have been granted a large stretch of land from Morocco and the Atlantic coast to most of Iraq on the border of Iran. The lands of Abraham's children other than Isaac and the lands formerly given to the descendents of Lot and of Esau have also been granted to Ishmael's descendents.

Nevertheless, Isaac, as the special son of promise through Abraham's wife Sarah, was the primary spiritual heir of Abraham and also the heir of the promised land itself. This promise passed to Jacob, not to Esau. For two consecutive generations God bypassed the oldest son in favor of a younger son, which offends most people's notion of what is natural and indeed is contrary to the human law of inheritance contained in the Law of Moses (Deuteronomy 21:17). This recurs with

Jacob's children, where Joseph became the heir with a double portion of land and Judah—the fourth oldest—became the man through whom the ultimate King of Kings would come. Justice is important in both Islam and Christianity, but in Christianity rigid justice is often set aside for divine mercy. "*Mercy and truth have met together; righteousness and peace have kissed each other.*" (Psalm 85:10). Our Lord Jesus upbraided the Pharisees for leaving out the great matters of the Law: "*justice, mercy and faith.*" (Matthew 23:23)

Let me add one further contrast. Judaism had set a precedent when their scholars in Alexandria had translated the Old Testament into Greek about 270 years before the Birth of Christ. The purpose of the translation was to make the Scriptures available in the language that people then used. By that time even many Jews were speaking Greek more than Hebrew. In the case of Christianity, the New Testament was translated from its original Greek into various languages long before Jerome made his translation into Latin that served Christians in the West for about 1000 years, into the time of Erasmus and Luther in the 1500s. During this time the Waldensians also had their version of the Bible. Luther translated the Vulgate into German. Tyndale and various Geneva-based scholars both translated the Bible into English and began to use the Greek text of Erasmus directly, climaxing with the Authorized Version of 1611. In the following years, publication of concordances spread the knowledge of the Biblical Greek to as many in the Christian church who were able and willing to read and study this material.

When the successors of Mohammed faced a similar problem with the Koran, they refused to permit translation because no translation into another language could precisely render the Koran from Arabic to another language. It is true that no translation from one language to another can be exact. But consider the consequences of the lack of an officially approved translation of the Koran as soon as Islam spread to people who did not know Arabic. During the time between the Council of Trent and Vatican Two, much the same situation existed in many Catholic parishes because Church doctrine forbade a lay person from possessing a Bible without special permission from a priest. Even before the Council of Trent, Luther possessed a Bible while a monk only because his monastic superior gave permission because of Luther's recurrent crises of conscience. In a Christian church, a pastor can be called to account if his preaching or his actions do not adhere to the Bible. The entire congregation has the Holy Scriptures in its possession, with resources linking the modern language translation to the original Greek. In a mosque, there was no parallel fund of knowledge in any congregation that did not have Arabic scholars. So the congregations became dependent on the imam to tell them what the Koran says. So in Islam, as in earlier times within the Catholic Church, there was an effective filter between their sacred writings and most people. People depended on their clergy to give more or less accurate explanations of the texts that they were supposed to follow. But in Biblical Christianity this has not been true. Notwithstanding the difficulties of precision posed by different languages, dating back to the Tower of Babel in Genesis 11:1-10, Biblical Christianity has labored to get the text of the Holy Bible into the hands of everyone who might read it and further has stressed literacy so that each believer could read the Scriptures for himself or herself. To take one historical example, the American Confederate General Stonewall Jackson risked prosecution under Virginia law forbidding the education of slaves before the American Civil War by teaching slave children to read the Bible.

To most Muslims, God is perceived as inscrutable and unknowable. Biblical Christianity takes a very different view. Both Abraham (Genesis 18) and Moses (Exodus 32) spoke directly with God. Moses was able to speak to Him without a veil (Exodus 34:34). As believers viewed as righteous through the blood of Jesus Christ, converted Christians, like Moses, can speak to God without a veil (2 Corinthians 3:18). We can be friends with God now (John 15:13-15) with perfect knowledge and intimacy after resurrection or rapture. 1 Corinthians 13:12, and consider also the picture of the Bride in Revelation 19. Paul's purpose was to *"know Him [Jesus Christ], and the power of His resurrection and the fellowship of His suffering, being made conformable to His death."* Philippians 3:10. Despite the vast gulf between, God can be known by human beings through the death and resurrection of Jesus Christ and His gift of the Holy Spirit.

Islam and Christianity have very different views of heaven. In Islam, one popular conception of heaven – at least for a man – is the presence of 72 curious virgins. This is primarily a concept of physical pleasure. Some Islamic scholars think that the verses in question are misunderstood, but I have tried to give a fair description of what appears to be a majority view. In Biblical Christianity, the primary concept of heaven is complete fellowship and union with God. Physical pleasure takes a secondary place. While Ephesians 5:22-33 does say that marriage is an analogy to the union between Jesus Christ and the believer in heaven, this union is not sexual. Bodies in heaven are very different and are *"neither marry nor are given in marriage."* Luke 19:35.

Most fundamentally of all, Islam and Christianity differ from one another over the identity of Jesus Christ. Islam agrees that the Lord Jesus was born of a Virgin Mary and was sinless. However, Islamic scholars balk at the Crucifixion. They believe that Judas or someone else died on the Cross instead of Jesus and that Jesus ascended into heaven without dying. Some then claim that Jesus will return to earth as a Muslim and help establish a renewed Islamic caliphate over the whole earth and then die. Christianity insists that Jesus Christ was fully man and fully God, that He died on the Cross as a Man as a ransom for the sins of many and that He rose from the dead the third day and 40 days thereafter ascended to heaven, never to die again. He will return and establish His own kingdom and reign with His Father in the Father's Kingdom forever. Philippians 2:5. In the meantime He is building His Church to share heaven with Him and with His Father and the Holy Spirit.

These views cannot both be true. Islam stresses the primacy of Mohammed as its prophet; Christianity stresses the worship of Jesus Christ as not only a prophet but as God in human flesh.

Q. Why do Christians oppose same-sex marriages? Aren't you discriminating? (a murmur of "Hear, hear" could be heard).

Yes, we are discriminating—between right and wrong. I am sure that none of you would have trouble putting a major Ponzi schemer in jail. Why does such a person lose his or her freedom? Because we realize that we must curtail the freedom of major criminals. No woman would be free if we let rapists roam at will. When Nazis unleashed the Gestapo against the Jews, the Jews lost their remaining freedom even before they were dragged to death camps. Anne Frank and many others had to stay hidden in attics or behind false walls. Denying freedom to persistent criminals is an essential part of preserving freedom for the general population. We can debate the details of capital punishment at another time, but at least in case of murder no punishment short of the death sentence is fully proportional to the injustice of murder.

Let me turn back to the original question with this foundation. Are same-sex marriages right or wrong? From the perspective of micro-evolution within a species, how many births have ever taken place by interaction between two males or two females? How can any species adapt with same-sex relations? Or consider the example of the original Creation. Same-sex sexuality was originally impossible because before the Fall there were only two human beings, one male and one female. Is not the Creation, preceding sin, an example for us set by God Himself? And why did Sodom and Gomorrah and their surrounding regions die in a day? Let me be clear: It is not same-sex practices alone that are evil, but all sexual relations outside of monogamous marriage. Heterosexual adultery is condemned in the Holy Bible in language rivaling the condemnation of same-sex practices and in the end has essentially the same awful result on Judgment Day, unless a particular person's sin of any type is forgiven through the saving blood of the Lord Jesus Christ.

Some people try to defend gay marriage by calling it love. Love in its highest form means self-sacrifice for the betterment of another, as the Lord Jesus sacrificed His life for the salvation of many. Love in a good marriage means that each partner sacrifices for the good of the other and that each partner encourages the other in doing good. Same-sex marriages parody this in that each partner encourages the other in committing evil. The degree of destruction in the region of Sodom and Gomorrah leaves no doubt as to the vehemence of God's anger at communities where same-sex relations were commonplace. Each partner is confirming the other in a mutual death spiral, not mutual love.

The effect is like two drowning people trying to hold on to one another under the surface. At the same time the whole idea of fatherhood, an important part of our knowledge of God, is also being confused.

We should also remember that not all that we call love is beneficial or holy. Love can be corrupted. The so-called love between Bonnie and Clyde was poisoned by their common objectives of robbery and murder. Comradeship and heroism is possible in an evil army like that of Nazi Germany as well as among Montgomery's soldiers. We cannot complement loyalty to Hitler, to Stalin or to Satan. A man may be enamoured with a woman while married to another, as was the poet Shelley. But such sentiment is wicked because misdirected contrary to the Word of God.

There is another aspect to your question. Through the grace and mercy of God I have been given the wonderful gift of everlasting life. The Bible has several categorical warnings—two of them are found in 1 Corinthians 6:9-11 and Revelation 22:15—that no person persistently and finally characterized by certain overt sins will enter the kingdom of God. Both heterosexual and same-sex sins are listed in those passages. Hebrews 11:6 informs us that *"with faith it is impossible to please Him."* Hebrews 12:14 tells us that *"without holiness no one will see the Lord."* John Bunyan wrote a profitable book based on 2 Timothy 2:19: *"Let everyone that names the name of Christ depart from iniquity."* I do not want to keep my wonderful gift to myself; I want to share it. In order to share that gift from God I am compelled to speak unpleasant truth. Right now some of you may hate me for it (*scattered boos along with others saying, "Let him finish."*). But none of us, whatever our particular propensities, can begin to understand the quality of the gift by Jesus Christ of His own life on behalf of sinners without some inkling of how evil we truly are. If I am to show love to you, I have to tell you the truth just as a doctor would have to tell you frankly if you had a serious or even fatal disease of the body. We all have been born with mortal bodies and correspondingly with souls that deserve everlasting punishment. Even one impure or evil thought is enough to make us unfit by nature to live in God's eternal presence.

I bear no ill-will or hatred toward any class of people and hope to show compassion to all. Were it not for the transforming mercy of God I would be worse. I echo the call of God through the Apostle Paul, *calling on all men everywhere to repent.* (Acts 17:30) But if we focus on the question originally asked, I defend the right of sensible governments to discriminate among people based on adherence to or violation of standards of essential right and wrong. I defend the duty of government to protect monogamous marriage for the sake of children and of all civilization. The essence of what modern governments can enforce can be found in the Fifth through the Ninth Commandments. As to the soul, no government can save anyone. Only Jesus Christ can do that.

Q. Why do Christians keep threatening people with hellfire?

The threat is real, not imaginary. Ezekiel repeated twice the duty of God's people to sound a warning, in Ezekiel 3 and 33. During the American Revolution, a note from a pro-British farmer to Colonel Ralls of the Hessian forces in Trenton was found in his pocket. It warned him of the approach of General Washington's troops. Apparently Colonel Ralls had never read it, and as a result he died and his force was destroyed. I have a duty from God to sound the warning of the fiery judgment to come. If a particular individual refuses to read the Bible's warning or hear my spoken warning or the warnings of others, that refusal falls on that person's head for all eternity. Especially in Matthew, the Lord Jesus repeatedly warned His hearers of the judgment to come. It is a sentry's grievous fault if he sees an enemy's movement and fails in his duty to warn. But you now have heard my warning and know where to find more information about the mortal threat to your souls and bodies. You are now responsible to heed God's warning from whatever source.

Q6. If God is the Creator, then why do genetic errors occur such as Downs Syndrome, Tay-Sachs and autism? Can't He prevent these things if He is so powerful? Or is He being cruel?

First, we must realize that the Creation we now observe is not the original perfect Creation but a version degraded by sin. As the Apostle Paul said in Romans 8:21-22, "*For the Creation itself shall be delivered from the bondage of corruption into the glorious liberty of the children of God. The whole Creation groans and travails in pain until now.*" The same is true of the human body. It is now mortal and subject to degradation and eventual decay. And we must remember that sin is an offense against an infinite God and therefore deserves an infinite punishment. Any misfortune we suffer on earth is less than what we deserve. As Paul said in Romans 6:23, "*The wages of sin is death.*" Misfortune for the rebel against God is a down payment on his or her wages, although it may alternatively serve as a spiritual wake-up call to bring a particular rebel to his or her senses and on to true repentance and faith in Christ Jesus. As a cross-reference, look up Isaiah 45:7.

Second, not all sickness and pain is a result of a particular sin or of God's peculiar displeasure. In John 9:2 dealing with a man born blind, Jesus Christ was asked, "*Who sinned, this man or his parents, so that he was born blind?*" In short, Jesus answered, "neither." In this case, the man was born blind for the glory of God—to be there for Jesus to heal. The man experienced the liberation of his body from physical blindness. More importantly, his soul was healed from spiritual blindness. I am thankful that most and probably all of you can see with your physical eyes. My prayer is that you will be given spiritual sight too.

In David's case, he lost four children because of his sin in having Uriah murdered in battle and then taking Uriah's wife Bathsheba as his own wife. David knew that after death he would see the baby who died when Bathsheba first gave birth. See 2 Samuel 12:23. Through family conflict David lost three other children. The children received no worse than they themselves deserved, and David was disciplined severely by God as a witness to God's displeasure with what David had done. Yet David's punishment did not even touch the normal penalty for David's sin—physical death followed by eternal punishment in the Lake of Fire.

David's family was one instance where a series of sins had terrible direct consequences. The Flood and the fire and brimstone of Sodom and Gomorrah were two other examples where particular sins provoked God to exemplary punishments of masses of people. But we cannot become judgmental and assume that a person who suffers has provoked the anger of God. Sometimes suffering is for the sake of the name of the Lord Jesus. As Peter puts it, "*It is better, if the will of God be so, that you suffer for well-doing than for evildoing.*" 1 Peter 3:17

God will eventually put an end to all death and pain for His people, and He will also administer perfect justice to those who have refused to surrender to His Son. Jesus Christ will deal with the souls of the disabled in precisely the right way. But we in faith must await His time for perfection to be ushered in.

Q7: I note that in your previous answer you mentioned the heroes of Scottish independence in the time of Bannockburn and of Protestant religious leaders, both Baptist and Presbyterian. Why did you omit Catholics or Orthodox people, among others?

I am not aiming to promote any particular denomination but I am a follower of Jesus Christ. I am blessed and humbled to have a direct relationship with Him, just as any person has who has been redeemed by His blood. There is a precise correspondence between Jesus Christ, the living Word of God in human flesh and now in a resurrected human body, and the written Word of God, the Holy Bible. In principle there is no place to require any doctrine or practice in His church which is not required or at least permitted by the Bible itself. We as fallible mortal men have no right or authority to change the directions of the living God. One of the Lord Jesus' most severe criticisms of the Pharisees was of their use of tradition to set aside the commands of God. You will find this in Matthew 15:1-9.

I can find much to admire in the individual lives of Francis of Assisi, Alexander Kolbe and of Mother Teresa. But when I compare the doctrines of liturgical churches that are offshoots of Christianity today with the Bible, those doctrines have the same essential flaw as the traditions of the Pharisees. For example, the Apostle Peter taught that all true believers were "a royal priesthood" (1 Peter 2:9). The book of Hebrews shows

Jesus Christ as the Great High Priest through Whom we all have access directly to the Father. We are commanded to come all the way to the Throne of Grace in our petitions for mercy and help in Hebrews 4:16. Then why does any church teach that a believing child of God must approach his or her Father through an earthly priest or through a deceased saint? And how can any portion of the free gift of eternal life described in Romans 6:23 be earned by a sinful mortal?

When the apostles themselves, Paul excepted (and Barnabas if he is counted as an apostle), were married men—and Peter was even called as a married man to be an apostle—how is it that any church has the right to insist that its parish clergy give up marriage and children? I know that the Pope of that day was trying to disentangle the clergy from power politics, but in attacking one issue he created a worse problem with repeated tragic results that still persist. And all because that Pope failed to obey the Scriptures, and in particular 1 Timothy 4:3 and the entire chapters of 1 Timothy 3 and Titus 1 about marriage being the norm for pastors.

The Apostle Paul is crystal-clear that as to salvation faith is the only way. The old Latin formula is that we are saved by grace alone through faith alone. Romans 2, 3 and 4 are especially directed at this. So are Romans 9 and 11, the first half of Galatians and Ephesians 1 and 2. Our works or attributes have nothing to do with salvation—they have much to do with sanctification once the Holy Spirit has started to work on our hearts and minds. So I cannot approve any assembly whose doctrines give partial credit to a human being for his or her salvation when in truth that salvation is the work of God and God alone. I love people within these assemblies and yearn that they will share my undeserved joy in learning the truth that they can relate directly to God as His child.

This sounds harsh, but bear with me. I am constrained to say this against my desire. Any human being will fall short of the glory of God, and no person's teaching, including mine, will even approach perfection. Any person who consciously rejects the Bible likewise rejects the God of the Bible. The entire concept that any person, church, religion or movement has any authority, source of doctrine or magisterium apart from or outside the Scriptures to deliberately create its own doctrine is anathema. The use of any source outside of Scripture as if it is equal or superior in authority to Scripture is an affront to the authority and majesty of God, even where the affront is unintentional and done in ignorance. The sin is far worse when the variation from the Bible is understood and deliberate. May God with His forgiving mercy bring us all from ignorance and rebellion to knowledge and to submission to His Word, both the written Word and the Living Word Jesus Christ.

In saying this, I should make a clear distinction between life on earth and life in heaven. On earth, it is essential for people of different faiths to coexist in peace, tolerating frank intellectual and spiritual debate. People of various faiths can be expected to evangelize those of other faiths, which is their right before human law. On earth religious freedom and debate is essential to civil society, which is ruled by fallible and sinful human beings. The Holy Spirit through Paul instructed Timothy and future pastors that *"the servant of the Lord must not strive, but be gentle to all. [He must be] apt to teach, patient, in meekness instructing those that oppose themselves, if God perhaps will give them repentance to the acknowledgement of the truth."* 2 Timothy 2:24-25.

By contrast to earthly society, in heaven where the holy God rules with His perfect Son Jesus Christ, there will be no diversity. "*Without faith it is impossible to please Him.*" Hebrews 11:6. I should point out that there is almost no sin on earth that some of the present and future citizens of heaven did not at one time love and practice. This is true alike of the sins of the body and of the mind and of combinations of both. The forgiveness of God is beyond human measure to any who will repent and believe. But since all citizens of heaven will be changed to be like Jesus Christ, their former diversity on earth will vanish.

Q8. Are you then advocating that God's people withdraw from the world, or else tyrannize everyone else because they know more?

Neither. Remember that believing Christians may know a little bit more because God has chosen to have mercy on them, not because they were intrinsically better. Ephesians 2 and 1 Corinthians 6 are emphatic that God's people were originally no better than anyone else. One almost cannot name a sin that has not at one time been practiced by people who later have become Christians through the mercy and power of God. There is no room in the Christian life for pride. Rather, humility is praised and pride is excoriated. Further, Jesus Christ rubbed shoulders with all kinds of people and His followers should follow that example. We are to be lights shining in the world, not hidden behind either literal or figurative walls.

No Christian can be born from above by human power, whether by huckster techniques or by brute force. Conversion comes from the Holy Spirit implantling into the human heart its initial initial expression of faith, followed by changes of heart and behavior. Christians do not seek dictatorship for themselves and fear dictatorial power in the hands of anyone. This has roots back to Samuel's warning against an absolute monarchy in 1 Samuel 8. For one illustration from English history, Cromwell was far more tolerant and self-controlled than either Charles I or Charles II, his predecessor and successor. And Winston Churchill, that redoubtable believer in political freedom and deadly foe of both Naziism and Communism, wrote of the night of Pearl Harbor that he "slept the sleep of the saved and thankful." [Winston Churchill, *The Grand Alliance,* p. 608, Houghton Mifflin Company, 1950] That sounds like a man who knew that he and his nation would be delivered by God, though not by man, whatever the immediate calamities may be.

Permit me one illustration concerning the tragedy of abortion. Christians can and should work wholeheartedly with people of many other faiths to try to stop the hemorrhage of human lives that are being taken daily. We cannot give up Biblical theology in the process, but we can and must work with people of varying beliefs for proper purposes within society. The same principle holds true in our workplaces and our military.

As to government, we are to seek to apply Christian principles to the issues of the day, but we are not to expect that Christians will lead secular governments for extended periods of time. Therefore, the powers of government must be limited carefully and kept in check vigilantly.

The people in charge of the hall are telling me that our time is up. I will be glad to meet with any or all of you who want to talk further if we can find a place. I also will be speaking down the street at this Sunday's service if you want to see me but cannot stay tonight.

One of the students suggested that everyone go to the pub across the street. Mr. Thomas said he would go and talk to anyone making sense but would not imbibe. A few people went; some really wanted to talk to him about his soccer background while others may have had some questions to clear up. So the meeting ended and most of the students, including Julie, filtered to their residences.

[For discussion, you can take up any one or more of the questions asked of Mr. Thomas if you wish.]

To her surprise, Julie thought there was something to what Mr. Thomas said. At first this may have been merely an opportunity to differ from her professors, but deep down she had long thought that there was more to life than the tooth and claw of evolution. Evolution cannot explain the forms of love apart from procreation, either among animals such as elephants or among human beings. Beyond that, she was not sure what she thought; Biblical Christianity as distinguished from a set of vague and sentimental traditions was new to her. She wanted some time to think. Then she decided to go to the church where Mr. Thomas would preach that Sunday. Julie was able to persuade several friends who had heard the Friday lecture to go with her. If nothing else, it was something to do and might make for a few laughs.

The service was strange to Julie at first. Although Julie had not been a churchgoer for several years, she was used to the more ceremonial forms of either a ceremonial Presbyterian or Anglican Church, what used to be called "High Church." In churches to which Julie had been exposed, the ceremonies were more important than the homily or congregational singing. So this was different. Now Julie was curious to hear what Mr.

Thomas had to say, so the unfamiliar more modernized singing neither excited nor bothered her. She wanted to get past this in order to concentrate on his sermon, which she expected to be different than anything she had heard before. In this she was not to be disappointed.

Part 1

Chapter 4

Sandy Thomas took the pulpit and mentioned his talk on Creation at the University the previous Friday night. He asked for prayer that the spiritual seed he had sown would bear fruit. Then he introduced his subject again as Creation, but this time he would focus on the importance of Creation as showing a God-given purpose for human beings. He opened with a Scripture reading from Revelation 4:11:

> *You are worthy, O Lord, to receive honor and*
> *glory and power;*
> *For You have created all things, and for Your*
> *pleasure they are and were created.*

The first concept that jumps out at us is that we were created by God for a purpose. We do not live at random or for no purpose.

On this level Darwin and all random evolutionists are completely wrong. Now before we take pride in the fact that we have a purpose from God, we need to remember that for those who rebel against God and refuse to repent His purpose is anything but enjoyable. Proverbs 16:4 warns us that *"The Lord has made all for Himself; yes, even the wicked for the day of evil."* Romans 9 informs us that the Lord raised up Pharaoh for the purpose of throwing him down to destruction. We need to plead with God to have mercy on us through Jesus Christ and grant us an undeserved purpose to be a companion of His forever.

But for those who believe, *"We are His workmanship created for good works, which God has before ordained that we should walk in them."* Ephesians 2:10. As the people of God, it is our responsibility to seek out and find those things for which God has prepared us and then obey Him in starting to perform. Once again we have the comfort of God's purpose as we toil.

Consider also the teaching about the gifts of the Holy Spirit in Romans 12:6: *"Having then gifts differing according to the grace that has been given to us . . ."* In Ephesians 4:11 one starts: *"And He gave some . . ."* In 1 Corinthians 12:4-6 we read, *"And there are diversities of gifts but the same Spirit. And there are differences of administrations but the same Lord. And there are diversities in operations but the same God Who works all in all."* In each passage God is the source of our abilities. We are not made by accident but according to divine purpose.

The Apostle Paul himself is a living example of that divine purpose. He introduces himself to the Galatians as *"Paul, an apostle not of men, neither by man, but by Jesus Christ and God the Father who raised Him from the dead . . ."* Galatians 1:1. Returning to this theme in Galatians 1:15-16, Paul wrote,

"But when it pleased God, Who separated me from my mother's womb and called me by His grace, to reveal His Son in me . . ." Paul was conscious of a special purpose of God for him. Even the timing of Paul's call was determined by God.

Queen Esther also had an unusual calling from God. She became the wife of Ahasuerus, also known as Xerxes, King of Persia. He did not realize that Esther was Jewish when he married her. You may remember that Haman decided to massacre all the Jews within the Persian Empire. This would have involved not only the capital city but the entire territory of Persia, including Jerusalem where a remnant of the exiles had returned and rebuilt the Second Temple. If successful, the plot would have wiped out the entire tribe of Judah and the entire priesthood, both crucial for future history. Remember Mordecai's challenge to Esther in Esther 4:14, *"For if you altogether hold your peace at this time, then shall enlargement and deliverance arise to the Jews from another place, but you and your father's house shall be destroyed.* Here is what I must emphasize: *"And who knows whether <u>you</u> are come to the kingdom for such a time as this?"*

You may not have been called to be a queen, but what about your present duties? Are you a parent, a student, a soldier? Are you a scientist, a teacher, a factory worker? Brother Andrew, who eventually became God's smuggler of Bibles behind the Iron Curtain, was a worker in a chocolate factory when he first showed his faith. Corrie ten Boom for years worked in her father's shop where watches were repaired. God's purposes for them were ripened while they did their jobs in obscurity. Did Susannah Wesley know that she was training one of the greatest evangelists known to history? Did Spurgeon's mother know that she was training a mighty preacher? At least not at first. They were faithful to the purpose of God revealed to them, and God's power multiplied their faithful labors the way the Lord Jesus multiplied the five barley loaves and two fish.

Ephesians 3:9-11 tells us that God has purposed that we illustrate for heavenly angels and principalities the wisdom of God. Speaking broadly, this can be accomplished in two ways. We can be people who shed light on what is right, or else we can be people who serve as examples of the consequences of unchecked sin. Jacob became, especially after he wrestled with the Son of God, an example of light and Esau was and remained an example of darkness. Moses was a child of light and Pharaoh was a child of darkness. No heavenly being could mistake the lesson of the ultimate deliverance of the righteous and the ultimate destruction of the wicked. Consider the gulf between the everlasting covenant between God and King David and his seed and the destruction of King Ahab and his seed. David's ultimate Seed was Jesus Christ, Who was crucified and Who rose from the dead. Ahab's wife and seed of 70 sons was wiped out at the instance of Jehu, an ancient real-life model for the modern fictional Terminator and also a preview of the Lord Jesus in His Second Coming. All this bloodshed fulfilled the prophecies of Elijah against Ahab by reason of Ahab and his wife Jezebel taking both life and land by false charges against Naboth. [1 Kings 21] The heavenly angels could readily observe the contrast in the ultimate consequences of good and evil, of submission to God or rebellion against Him, from their vantage point in the heavens. With the aid of the written Bible, so can we. It is not that we can earn God's favor or make ourselves righteous. Only the Holy Spirit can change our naturally evil characters, and then we can begin to become righteous though we will always fall short of God's standards in this life. Like David, we too have a great cloud of witnesses who learn from us one way or the other. Hebrews 12:1 says, "*Considering that we are surrounded by such a great cloud of witnesses, let us lay aside every weight, and the sin which so easily besets us. Let us run with endurance the race that is set before us."*

None of us have the same call as Paul did. But in principle every Christian is the same in that God has a special purpose in calling us to Himself. If you do not yet believe in Jesus Christ, then ask Him to send His Holy Spirit and reveal good purposes for you. Then ask Him to start changing you so that you can get ready for those good purposes. Right now your purpose may center on your work, your education or your family. In time your purpose should grow. Think back to the passages we mentioned earlier on the gifts of the Holy Spirit. "*There are differences in administration but the same Lord."*

You may still doubt that God has a special purpose for you. But He Himself has said so, and you can trust His word to be true. There is one more Scripture that comes to mind to clinch this. Read Romans 8:28: "*And we know that all things work together for good to them that love God, who are called according to . . . .* ***purpose***. We know that we have a purpose from God. Let us go forward and meet it with confidence in Him and in His Son Jesus Christ!

Let us pray: Lord Jesus, reveal your purposes to each believer here and use your Holy Spirit to drive us forward in joy to serve you in the good works that you have designed for us. In Jesus' name, Amen.

When the congregation went home, the girls went to the nearest snack bar to dissect Mr. Thomas' sermon, with "roast preacher" on the side. Julie ventured that he displayed a definite purpose and apparently believed what he said. So many of the other boys that they knew were floundering as they studied without a plan or long-range purpose. Her friends disagreed. One said, "I don't want a man like him telling me what to do or whom to worship, if anyone. I want to be my own person. Even if I marry I do not want to belong to someone else."

Julie rejoined, "So you don't believe that marriage is permanent?" The other girl responded, "No. One man may work for me in my twenties but another in my forties. Why should I not be free to change?"

Julie asked, "But what if your husband still enjoys living with you?"

The girl answered, "So what! If he doesn't please me any more, I have every right to move on."

Another said, "He preaches as if God owns us. Well, I don't like it. Nobody owns me. God didn't even make me—my parents did. Whether that was smart or not I'm not sure. But we all live with the consequences of the decisions of others, not just our own. That's not fair but that's the way it is."

Julie remembered that Shakespeare wrote and quoted him, "'To be or not to be, that is the question.' But the preacher says that we don't have that option. What we might control temporarily is the state of our being, whether in our human body or in another state. A person who commits suicide kills the body but cannot stop the existence of the soul. We will always exist; we will always be conscious. But will we be happy?"

A third girl chimed in, "How are we supposed to be happy? We are in a constant evolutionary struggle to obtain resources and then to procreate after our kind. The way men are today they can't be trusted. They are 'hit-and-run' artists who get us pregnant and then make us chase them to get some support in raising the children. What good are they?" (For a further discussion on the nature of leadership and masculinity, you may turn to Appendix A at this point.)

Julie asked, "Do you think the preacher is like that?"

The third girl responded, "I don't know him personally but I doubt if he is any different when you get underneath what he says to how he lives. Men are all the same." The other girls nodded in agreement and then the discussion broke up.

As Julie went home, the cynicism of the other girls nagged at her. If they were right, happiness is indeed virtually impossible whether married or unmarried. Moreover, Julie was not convinced that consciousness ceases at physical death. She knew that ancient religions such as those of Greece and Egypt and more modern religions such as those of the Orient all agree that consciousness continues after physical death, although they disagree on the particulars. Emotionally, Julie desired a purpose. In response to what the last girl said, her first thought was to try to investigate Mr. Thomas as much as she could, as would a biologist, to see whether he lived the way he talked. So she started to investigate his history and also to learn something about his schedule so that she could observe him *incognito*.

The Internet provided Julie with a good start. Piecing together information from newspapers, and social websites, she was able to trace Sandy's basic schedule as a teacher, football coach, speaker and lecturer. There was no obvious deviation from what he professed in his two talks. For example, there were no instances of drunkenness or boasts of sexual conquests. Unlike many profiles, there was no astrology. (Later Julie would learn that the Bible forbids astrology, most directly in Isaiah 47:13.) Julie did note casually that he was single, as she suspected. There were a few Bible verses and some sketchy biographical material. In the main, Sandy seemed definitely masculine without being wild or uncontrolled. Julie did not see anything so far to justify the cynicism of her friends, but she was still scratching the surface.

Of all the times on his schedule when Sandy would be open to observation without his knowing it, football practice with his teen-age team had the best promise of giving Sandy rope to reveal his true colors. He would be in a male and physical environment that might make Sandy think that he has liberty to be loose with his language. He would have authority—if he were inclined to be abusive to those beneath him, the stress of a football practice should be a good place for that characteristic to show itself. There would be no restraining influence of a referee or of his assistants. If the team members were afraid of his anger, it would show in their body language. So Julie located the practice field and observed from a distance.

To her surprise, the practice was intense but without the cussing normally associated with English football. Sandy corrected his players without harsh language or screaming above the level necessary to bridge the distance between coach and player. There was no question that he was in charge. Sandy was direct in both praise and criticism. Yet the young men seemed comfortable, neither cringing nor rebellious. Julie had never seen conditioning this rigorous before, but Sandy participated with the rest of the team. That seemed to make the hard demands of football more bearable. So she decided to continue her investigation from a distance.

Part 1

Chapter 5

From his Facebook site Julie learned that Sandy was giving another speech before a city-wide Christian youth gathering, so she arranged to attend. As before, Sandy tied his teaching to Creation, but this time his focus was on the connection between the teaching of Creation and the teaching of the resurrection of the dead:

I am fully aware that your teachers are instructed to teach as if the random evolution of nature leading to human beings is an undisputed fact. In one sense they are just doing their jobs, although in the process they are leading youth astray. In previous recent teaching I have gone into detail about how nature is orderly and not random, and that therefore one should logically conclude that nature is not the product of a random process. To take one example, we know that given the atmosphere of the earth one can either breathe in carbon dioxide and exhale oxygen or the reverse. If the process were random we would expect to find animals and plants using each method. But that is not what we find. We observe that animals breathe in oxygen and exhale carbon dioxide, while plants breathe in carbon dioxide and exhale oxygen. This keeps the atmosphere from running out of oxygen which humans beings and other animals need to live. It also is evidence of intelligent engineering and design, since plants use one method and animals the other. There are many other cases where life forms that are quite different nevertheless depend on one another and could not have come into existence independent of one another. To take one example, how could tiny disease-causing microbes survive without human or other animal hosts in which to multiply? Indeed, what of other microbes which benefit human beings and live in their intestines? Nature is not random but is carefully designed like an old-fashioned Swiss watch made by a master watchmaker. The whole concept of a "blind watchmaker" bringing about our complex, balanced environment is absurd.

Let me explain. Suppose we have two blind people who are each supposed to make a functional and durable watch. The first was trained as a watchmaker and lost his sight late in life, but still has his memory and knows the feel of each part of the watch. My comparison gives the evolutionist too much of an advantage in assuming that the pre-cut parts of the watch are actually there and within reach. That's like assuming that you can assemble the computer and have it work without installing the operating system. But we can by-pass that for sake of illustration. The second blind man never has made or even seen a watch but has an identical bag of components and tools available to him. At the end of the exercise, each has put the parts inside a case. Which watch would you buy if you had to choose one? Obviously, you would choose the watch assembled by the man who understands the design and purpose of a watch. By analogy, I am asking you to believe that human beings and indeed all of nature are designed with definite purposes. Random evolution is important when considering the history of ideas, and it indeed would be instructive to trace how evolutionary theory has itself evolved over time from Darwin to today. But as a scientific theory random evolution is nonsense in the face of the orderliness and balance of nature even in its fallen condition after sin and death entered the universe.

But there is a greater reason why random evolution should be regarded as fable rather than fact. If we bypass all scientific arguments against random evolution for discussion's sake, we have still another problem in that random evolution and resurrection are incompatible. If resurrection is true, random evolution must be false.

If one tests the hypothesis that human beings are the product of random evolution, it must be admitted that somehow human beings as well as other forms of life on earth acquired the characteristic of mortality. We die, even if we do not fall victim to predators. We have discovered some corpses several thousand years old. Some were in Pharaohs' tombs. One was preserved in a Danish peat bog. Another was frozen in the Austrian Alps. We know that these people have not experienced a bodily resurrection because their bodies are still here and would decay if permitted. The same is true of the body of Lenin in Russia. This tells us two things: (1) That resurrection is not an inherent characteristic intrinsic to human beings; and (2) That the dead were not able to move, eat or use any objects which were left for their use after death, as in ancient Egyptian beliefs. If the resurrection of dead human beings will take place, it must be through a power outside the human race. That same power would logically be our Creator.

Now proceed to the most critical question: will you personally rise from the dead? The Bible leaves no doubt. For example, Daniel 12:2 says, "*Many of them that sleep in the dust of the earth shall awake—some to everlasting life and some to shame and everlasting contempt.*" Job also knew of his coming resurrection, as he expressed it in Job 14:14 and in Job 19:23-27. David understood, as Psalm 16 shows. The Lord Jesus strongly affirmed that human beings will be raised from the dead. For example, in John 5:28-29 He said this: "*For the hour is coming in which all who are in the graves shall hear His voice and shall come forth, those that have done good to the resurrection of life and those who have done evil to the resurrection of damnation.*" I would note briefly that Romans 3:9-18 tells us that no person outside of the transforming power of God has done good, so this text expresses a test of evidence rather than the idea that anyone can earn salvation on our merit when in fact we have no merit on our own. But to the main issue now in focus, there can be no question that Jesus Christ taught the universal resurrection of the dead. As a matter of human choice you might disbelieve Him, but no one can argue that Jesus Christ Himself did not believe in life after physical death, in the resurrection and in the judgment. If you have any lingering doubt on that score, review Luke 16:19-31, Luke 20:27-38 and Matthew 25:31-46.

I realize that many of you would rather live your life as you please and then go on to perpetual sleep, never to be bothered by God or anyone else. But you do not get that option. In September 1939, no resident who remained in Poland was able to escape the alliance of Stalinist Russia and Nazi Germany.

There is a perpetual war between God and Satan in process right now, and you and I are in the battle zone and cannot escape the conflict. This is a prime cause of death. Revelation 12 makes it clear that the theater of this war is the entire universe. The Apostle Paul even agreed in 1 Corinthians 15:32 that if there is no resurrection of the dead that hedonism is logical. But if there is no resurrection from the dead, there is no moral accountability, no enduring love and no long-run purpose for humanity. If you take a choice of perpetual sleep, you would be a fool because you would miss the opportunity of everlasting love and fellowship with Jesus Christ beyond physical death and the grave. That is your great opportunity for never-ending, boundless joy.

But in fact perpetual sleep is not an option. Some of you may remember how your parents insisted that you wake up for school, for work or for some other obligation when you wanted to sleep in your bed. As Hebrews 9:27 says, *"It is appointed to man once to die, and after this the judgment."* We have already referenced Matthew 25:31-46, in which Jesus Christ explains that everlasting judgment includes everlasting punishment. Other Scriptures make it clear that everlasting fire and everlasting darkness are two of the components of this everlasting judgment. You may be able to sleep through almost anything, but you will not sleep through the judgment, nor will you get any rest if you are sentenced to everlasting judgment. The human race in the end will realize that eternity cannot be avoided, but the knowledge will be too late to do any good. Consider how men and women as predicted in Revelation 6:15-17 will cry out for the rocks and hills to fall on them and cover them in the vain hope that they might be hidden from the wrath of the aroused Lamb of God.

Human beings were created with purpose. Adam and Eve originally enjoyed the presence of God, and through the blood-sacrifice of the Lord Jesus Christ, the combined Son of God and Son of Man, you can enjoy fellowship with God in all His fullness forever. God offers you heaven through faith or hell through unbelief or neglect, and every human being ever conceived will know one or the other. But this capacity to live after the death of the body is not the product of evolution but the design of God as Creator. We are not the product of random evolution but of purposeful Creation. I call on each of you to stop defending your individual brand of sin, whatever it may be, and instead ask God to change you according to His loving purpose through faith in Jesus Christ as God and Man in one Person. Right now God offers you mercy. Remember John 3:16: "*For God so loved the world that He gave His only begotten Son, that whosoever believes in Him should not perish but have everlasting life.*"

The format of this meeting did not allow for questions later. Julie had taken some notes about the Scripture references Sandy had cited and looked them up. She found his references to be accurate and the texts troubling. Her previous brushes with religion did not prepare her for either an offer of eternal life or a warning of eternal punishment. But she did think that Sandy's attacks on random evolution were logical and in conformity with what scientists can actually observe. After all, Linnaeus' classification system matches a structure existing in nature. Julie also had a pang of conscience that men and women needed a greater purpose than self-aggrandizement or even the preservation of a family group or clan, which is the logical outcome of evolutionary theory. Idealism makes no sense in an evolutionary world, but idealism properly channeled is necessary for human society and progress. So Julie decided to continue to watch Sandy from a distance and wait for another opportunity for some real contact with him. In the meantime, she did see on the Internet that he would be a substitute preacher at another church the following Sunday. So she went to learn and observe more.

QUESTIONS FOR REFLECTION & DISCUSSION:

1. How important is the doctrine of Creation to Christianity?
2. Why is death universal, except for those translated directly to the presence of God such as Enoch and Elijah and those yet to be translated (1 Corinthians 15:51-53)?
3. How important is the doctrine of bodily resurrection to Christianity?
4. Peter in Acts 2 pointed to the empty tomb 50 days after the Resurrection of Jesus Christ as evidence of His resurrection? Are you persuaded? Why or why not?
5. How can a Christian fight pride in his own heart and mind? If there is any doubt about the terribly sinful nature of pride, do a word study on pride in Proverbs.

Part 1

Chapter 6

Alexander Thomas mounted the pulpit and announced his subject as the book of Jonah:

You may wonder why I am teaching from such a short and relatively unknown portion of the Scriptures. My attention was directed when I read that J.P. Morgan, the great American financier of the early 20th century, had made this his favorite book of the Bible and often asked his daughter to read it to him during his declining days on earth. His name is still remembered in two great corporations: J.P. Morgan Chase and Morgan Stanley. Obviously he was an intellectually vigorous man and once was able to step before the investing public and stop a financial panic. While J.P. Morgan did not always behave as a Christian during his youth and middle age, he was an outspoken Christian during his later years and gave one of the most remarkable testimonies in favor of the Christian faith in his will. You can still find it on the Internet today. J.P. Morgan in his own time and at his death was one of the very wealthiest men that has ever walked the earth, but he advised his posterity and the entire world that his most precious legacy by far was faith in Jesus Christ for the salvation of souls, including his own. If the book of Jonah was his favorite book, it stands to reason that it is worth a fresh examination. There is far more to it than Jonah being swallowed by the great fish, although that is an important part of the book.

My basic theme here in St. Andrews has been God as Creator. Jonah actually fits the theme in the 1st chapter. The portrayal of God there is incompatible with any idea of evolution. God not only created the heavens and the earth, but He also intervenes according to His own will to change the natural course of events. The people of Nineveh would not normally hear anything about the God of Abraham, Isaac and Jacob, so God commanded Jonah to go and tell them and also warn them to repent because His judgment was about to fall on them. In relation to Nineveh, this message is also found later in Nahum. Jonah resided in the Northern Kingdom, which during his time was under growing pressure from Nineveh. In fact Jonah may well have foreseen that Nineveh and the Assyrian Empire would eventually destroy the Northern Kingdom. In any case Jonah wanted no part of warning the Assyrians away from God's judgment.

Did Jonah's will stop God? Not in the slightest! Jonah had enough money to pay for passage to an area on the east coast of modern Spain, on the other side of the Mediterranean from Nineveh on the upper Tigris River in modern Iraq. Jonah got on the boat and it cast off. He went to sleep below decks. Jonah thought that he had put God's commission out of his picture.

But then God sent a storm to make it impossible for the ship to make headway and indeed threatened to sink the vessel. When the ship's company cast lots to determine who was the cause of the trouble, God made sure that the lots correctly identified Jonah (see Proverbs 16:33) as the source of the trouble. Jonah confessed and gave permission for the crew to throw him overboard.

The crew had compassion on Jonah and tried to reach land, but God did not allow it. One might expect that God would now allow Jonah to reach land and belatedly start on his assigned mission. Instead God made sure that Jonah was thrown into the sea for His correction and chastening first. The men finally threw Jonah into the sea when there was nothing else to be done. When they did, the storm ceased immediately. Then a great fish came and swallowed Jonah and carried him down to the depths of the sea.

In terms of God's control over His Creation, note that God gave a message to His chosen prophet Jonah. When Jonah disobeyed, God stopped Jonah's flight by His control over weather and sea. Then he sent the fish to the exact right place—no need for GPS with God—at the exact right time to swallow Jonah. God was in control and exercised that control from start to finish. In chapter 4 one will see the exact same pattern with the gourd and the worm that killed the gourd, all to teach Jonah and all of us the lesson that each soul is precious.

We cannot bypass the severity of God's chastening and discipline of Jonah. Sometimes a loving parent must be severe. Being thrown into the heaving sea is bad enough. But imagine being in the belly of the great fish. There would be no light there. Jonah apparently was in pitch darkness for three days and three nights. Who can say what sensations Jonah felt as the great fish changed its direction in the ocean depths. If any of you has ever flown in an unpressurized airplane, you might have some idea. Jonah might have been either hot or cold and the oxygen may well have been depleted. If you know someone who fought in diesel submarines, he could give you an earful of what it was like. Jonah might have been banged from side to side as the fish turned and he would have no advance notice of when the turns would come. He might have been flipped upside down. It would have been a non-stop, nauseating roller-coaster ride. Who know what liquids Jonah might have felt or tasted down there. One lesson you can learn from Jonah: if you are thinking about disobeying God deliberately, don't go there! The chastening was not the end of Jonah's story, but it must have been an experience that Jonah never forgot any more than a prisoner would forget incarceration. Listen to David's plea after his own experience with disobeying God as he expressed it in Psalm 32:9: *"Do not be like the horse or the mule which have no understanding, whose mouth must be held with bit and bridle, lest they come near you."*

When you read the prayers that Jonah offered from within the great fish, you can realize that Jonah did get the message. His prayers were full of references to the Psalms, showing that Jonah was a close student of the Scriptures that were then available. This is a second great lesson from Jonah: no matter how deep you are enmeshed in sin, if you have faith even in the horrible situation that you yourself have caused, God does hear the prayer of the broken and contrite heart, as David reminds us in Psalm 32:5 and especially in Psalm 51:17. Jonah learned from experience the lessons of these psalms, both of the horror of sin and the pain of God's correction, but also of the glorious mercy of God's forgiveness. Jonah did have to endure one final indignity: being vomited from the belly of the great fish with sundry liquids and debris to dry land. I have no clue how Jonah smelled or in what condition his clothes were in, but he must have been a frightful sight. He certainly was in no shape for a date (*chuckles*)!

When God repeated His command to Jonah, this time Jonah obeyed and indeed that generation of Ninevites repented. Even the king took off his finery and wore sackcloth, sitting in ashes. The king's sense of sin was so strong that he commanded everyone to abstain not only from food but from water for 3 days. The city was spared near-certain destruction!

But Jonah was unhappy. He would rather have seen a fireworks show like Sodom and Gomorrah than mercy shown to Nineveh. Sometimes we rub shoulders with people whose sins are so aggravating that we would rather see them judged than saved. We cannot go there because we deserve God's wrath ourselves. In the New Testament we are told to love our enemies (Matthew 5:44, Luke 6:27-28, 35) and to do good to them (Romans 12:20). We may have trouble with this as Jonah did, but we must go forward. I think of the historical example from America when the great general Stonewall Jackson prayed for the soul of John Brown, who sought to incite a slave insurrection and was hanged, the night before Stonewall commanded troops that were at the gallows.

You may be curious as to whether I believe that Jonah was actually swallowed by a great fish, whether a whale or a similar large sea creature. I do believe it because Jesus Christ said so. We find in Matthew 12:39-41 that the Lord Jesus referred to the "sign of the prophet Jonah," which referred to Jonah's time in the great fish as a sign of His time in the grave. He also warned His contemporaries in Israel that the repentant Ninevites would be saved even as Gentiles and that the majority of Jesus' contemporary countrymen were headed for perpetual damnation. Since the Lord Jesus said that the event was real, let us take His word for it. Both stubborn Jonah and the Ninevites found mercy from God through repentance and faith, as did also the ship's crew. The death of the perfect Son of God and Son of Man is payment for all sin for those who repent and believe. His resurrection is proof that God the Father accepted the payment. I plead with you also to *"Seek the Lord while He may be found; Call on the Lord while He is near. Let the wicked forsake his way and the unrighteous man his thoughts. And let him return to the Lord, and He will have mercy on him, for He will abundantly pardon."* (Isaiah 55:6-7) Come to the Lord in repentance and faith and so pass from eternal death to eternal life. Even King Manasseh, the worst of Judah's kings for most of his reign, found mercy when He repented and prayed to God from an Assyrian jail (2 Chronicles 33:11-13). You too will find mercy. As Paul wrote in Romans 10:13, *"Whosoever will call on the Lord shall be saved."* And again as Isaiah wrote, *"Though your sins be as scarlet, they shall be as white as snow. Though they be as crimson, they shall be as wool."* (Isaiah 1:18) As I pray in closing, call upon Him now!

Julie recognized that the Christianity she was hearing from Mr. Thomas was quite different from anything she had heard either in her previous exposures to church or at the university. To her it was radically new. She drew no immediate conclusions but once again did read the Book of Jonah and the other references that Mr. Thomas made.

QUESTIONS FOR DISCUSSION & REFLECTION:

1. Is Jesus' statement enough for you to believe that the events in the Book of Jonah actually took place?
2. Compare God's calming the Mediterranean Sea here with Jesus Christ's calming the Sea of Galilee in Matthew 14:32.
3. How does the Book of Jonah compare with Matthew 10:29?
4. Can we explain why the generation of Nineveh contemporary with Jonah received God's mercy while most of the generation of Israel contemporary with the Lord Jesus refused His message and instead received the judgment of God? For the basic fact, consult Matthew 12:39-42. What were the differences between the responses of the Ninevites to Jonah's preaching and the responses of Israel's leaders (with few exceptions) to the preaching of the Lord Jesus? Were the differences in the responses because the Ninevites were good and the Israelites bad? Consider Ephesians 2 as you answer.

Part 1

Chapter 7

Julie had heard Sandy three times and had observed him from a distance. She remained intrigued with this man that seemed so different from her fellow male students. Julie always tended to be mature, and certainly the death of her mother and Julie's efforts to help her father through his grief accelerated that maturation. But with that maturation came a desire to complete her studies and to settle down into a job or perhaps into marriage. The example of Julie's parents' long and monogamous marriage had rubbed off on her.

So Julie took another step and sent questions to Sandy by the Internet. One of them asked for recommended materials for further study of Creation. Another asked about references for Bible study materials. She also challenged his apparent belief in a literal, physical resurrection expressed in his Jonah sermon as old-fashioned. Julie's motives were mixed; her questions were genuine but she also wanted to work to a personal meeting without being too forward. She was concerned that Sandy was too concerned with his work to be able to notice her personally. Although Julie did not know this, she was beginning to behave in a modern setting much like Ruth in an ancient Jewish agricultural society in going to sleep on Boaz's threshing floor. Along with Julie's self-imposed project she was also completing her undergraduate biology studies and was ready to graduate. Sandy had found more material for her and responded in some detail about Creation and the resurrection:

"Dear Julie, Permit me to add a personal note about Creation and evolution in addition to the materials and links I am sending in response to your questions. The more we learn about the universe, the more improbable random evolution looks because even the smallest particles and life forms appear to be more and more complex. That means that human beings are many megnitudes more complex than Darwin could have realized, with a corresponding decline in the probability of random evolution.

It also occurs to me that the principle of redundancy in the human body points to design rather than evolution. We have two eyes and two ears, whereas evolution would require only one of each. We have two lungs and two kidneys where one would be sufficient for life. Parts of our brain can be retrained to take over for portions of the brain damaged by trauma. Our bodies go far beyond the minimum requirements for survival and reproduction, indicating an conscious design to guard against fatal consequences of a failure of any one part of the body.

Suppose I am strapping cargo to the top of my car. I would design two straps to hold every item in place, in case one fails, so as to avoid causing an accident and losing the cargo by the failure of a single strap. This redundancy in the fastening is evidence of intelligent design, although in my case that intelligence might be minimal. It certainly excludes randomness. I am extending this principle to nature itself. No evolutionary theory can account for redundancy.

Biblical Creation not only explains redundancy, but it explains light, gravity and water as well. Random evolution has no explanation for any of these basic necessities of earthly life. The Holy Scriptures simply identify God as the Creator of light (Genesis 1:3) and also identify Jesus Christ as the One Who exerts the force of gravity at its precisely calibrated intensity (Colossians 1:17; consist=hold together). God and the Holy Spirit are both identified as being connected with the newly created water. (Genesis 1:2,6-9) Most random evolutionists for pride's sake (like Henley, "I am the master of my fate, I am the captain of my soul") are atheists or want to be atheists against the testimony of their own consciences.

The Bible was not written to be a scientific textbook, but it does give us an opening to scientific understanding within limits. Look also at Job 38-41 and Job's right reaction in Job 42 when Job realized how limited his knowledge really was. Even with our modern increase in knowledge prophesied by Daniel (12:4), we still cannot answer on the basis of scientific knowledge many of the questions that God asked Job. On earth, we will never know what He knows. But we are created with a divine purpose.

Your question about resurrection goes to the very heart of the Bible and of genuine Christianity. This issue of bodily resurrection divided the Jewish contemporaries of the Lord Jesus and seemed absurd to most Greeks even though Greek myths did teach an afterlife. But our Lord Jesus used very strong language in rebuking the Saducees who did not believe in resurrection. "*You do err, not knowing the Scriptures nor the power of God.* (Matthew 22:29) Our Lord went on to quote from God's announcement to Moses at the burning bush. "*I am the God of Abraham, of Isaac and of Jacob.*" Then He gave the devastating rejoinder concerning His Father: "*He is not the God of the dead but of the living.*" In John 5:28-29 our Lord plainly taught that every human being—both the good and the evil—who has lived will be raised from the dead. So it is impossible to follow Jesus Christ if one denies the resurrection of the dead. In fact Job (14:14, 19:23-27), David (Psalm 16), Isaiah (26:19) and Daniel (12:2-3) all affirmed the resurrection of the dead in the Old Testament.

The Apostle Paul especially emphasized the resurrection of the dead. The most detailed treatment is 1 Corinthians 15. Paul also mentioned it in various speeches recorded in Acts 13:29-39, 17:31-32, 23:6, 24:15 and 26:23. I am sure that Paul spoke of it far more in speech not recorded in Scripture.

The truth of the resurrection of the dead is critical as a motivation for Christian ethics. Paul in 1 Corinthians 15:32-33 admitted that there is no point in living a virtuous life if there is no resurrection from the dead. Our Lord Jesus taught a system of eternal rewards for faithfulness now in Matthew 25:14-30, mentioned also with a slight variation in Luke 19:13-27. Note also our Lord's promise of rewards in heaven found in Matthew 19:29-30 and the mention of mansions in John 14:2-3. This is far from exhaustive, but it is sufficient to prove that the Lord Jesus taught the resurrection of the dead. If you believe in Him, this should be sufficient to settle your heart and mind about eternity to come."

{For discussion & reflection: At this point you may wish to discuss Creation and the importance of the bodily resurrection of the Lord Jesus and also the doctrine of bodily resurrection of all human beings, considering 1 Corinthians 15, Luke 24, Matthew 28, Mark 16 and John 20 and also Psalm 16, Daniel 12, Isaiah 26:19, Job 14:10-22, 19:23-27; and Revelation 20.}

Later that day Julie asked by e-mail if she could ask some questions in person. Her request was genuine but at the same time Julie wanted an opportunity to spend some time personally to size Sandy up. So Julie asked for her appointment and suggested that they go to a booth at the nearby snack bar after a practice later in the week. Sandy had some unscheduled time and agreed. Each got a soda and awkwardly looked at each other for a moment.

So Julie asked Sandy, "I know very little about football. Tell me about the game that made you famous."

Sandy started, I was goalkeeper for the Penzeance Privateers, a league 12 side. I was 22 then. We had a very young, inexperienced team. We had already done more than expected to survive into the third round when the Premier League teams of England join the FA Cup draw. As providence would have it, our team drew the Manchester Fusion, an absolute powerhouse and a contender to win both the Premier League and the Champions League of the best teams in Europe. Viewed in terms of the natural ability of the two sides, this was an absolute mismatch."

Julie asked, "Why Privateers?"

Sandy explained, "You have probably heard of the Gilbert and Sullivan operetta 'The Pirates of Penzeance.' The team did not want to call themselves pirates, but in fact maritime raiders were based there. Privateers held Letters of Marque that authorized them to fight legally on behalf of the English government instead of as pirates with authority from nobody. They divided prize money with the Crown. But English raiders from Penzeance had had a good deal more success than the modern football team. That is why so many raw, young players were brought in. There was nothing to lose.

Julie interjected, "So this was something like David and Goliath?"

Sandy returned, "Not remotely to the same extent. David versus Goliath was a struggle for the future of civilization, although people can only realize that looking over centuries of Bible history. And Goliath was killed, but Man Fusion survived to play in other competitions and has done quite well. Perhaps losing to Penzeance spurred them on. Although it was not obvious at the time, upon David's victory hinged about half of the Book of Psalms, the establishment of Israel as a kingdom for about 4 centuries and a long line of posterity that includes Kings Solomon, Hezekiah and Josiah, the prophet Zephaniah and climaxes with Joseph the legal, adoptive father of the Lord Jesus, the Virgin Mary through a different line of descent from David, and as to His humanity Jesus Christ Himself. If you change that one encounter to the expected result that Goliath killed David instead of the actual result, human history would be drastically different and very much worse."

Julie responded, "I want to hear more about that, but right now I want to hear more about your own moment of fame. I know your team won, but how?"

Sandy answered, "To start, there was no single miracle. There were several providential factors that narrowed the effect of the talent gap. Some of the Fusion's very best players were rested because of their long season in both English and European competition. Normally, putting out their very best team in that game would be like getting a sledgehammer to kill a fly. Using some second-line players is common and necessary during the long season. We, of course, put out the best we had. It was a very cold and windy day, perhaps -5° at kickoff and probably colder at the finish. The field was hard although playable. The wind was gusting between 15 and 30 miles per hour, blowing diagonally across the field. I must admire the hardy fans of Penzeance that filled our little stadium to a capacity of 5000. Oddly enough, someone had bought the naming rights for a small fee and named it Resurrection Stadium. The fans were loud for such a number. Perhaps our young players—about half of them were in their late teens—were less bothered by the cold and wind and less prone to muscle pulls. But none of these things, even in combination, explain the result. On rare occasions God for His reasons chooses to put His thumb on the scales to produce a nearly impossible result. This was one of them."

Julie said, "What about your part? What did you do to become famous?"

Sandy continued, "I did probably play the game of my life. The wind made long balls difficult to control and to predict. Many Man Fusion attempts to spring a player behind our defense during the first half was blown too far either out of play or into a place where I could field it directly. This helped our coach's strategy to play an offside trap and challenge the Fusion players for possession whenever possible as opposed to packing our players into our own defensive penalty area. They had the wind advantage in the first half and had trouble adjusting. We did our best to deny them time to get comfortable control, although during the first half we mounted no attack into the wind. For my part, I roamed throughout the large goal area to snag high balls before they bounced. From my vantage, I seemed to get a better view than the Fusion attackers, so I was able to get prime position to snuff out attacks before they got started. Fortunately for us, the few direct long-distance attempts on goal that I could not reach were too high. I did have two or three good saves.

Then we had the wind diagonally behind us in the second half. At least I could properly clear our area when we had a goal kick. The Fusion still had more chances than we did because they were fundamentally better players, but at least there was a bit more balance because of the wind. But nobody had scored and the game was near the end of stoppage time when our side was awarded a free kick just past the center circle on the right. Coach had said to go all-out to win instead of playing for a tie, which would have meant a replay at the Fusion stadium and virtually certain defeat. So I sprinted forward to take the free kick myself and yelled and signaled for everyone on our team to go forward. I wanted one last crack if there were a few seconds left. Instead of aiming directly at the center of their goal, I kicked toward the near post with a right-to-left swerve. The diagonal wind added to the swerve and carried the ball from the near post across the goal and well past the far post. One of our players had the foresight to move up wide on our left and had a running header moving into the ball about 12 yards from the goal line. He headed it back across the goal and out of the reach of their keeper, who had moved to the far post to guard against a possible direct header. He stumbled slightly as he tried to scramble back toward the near post, and we had two players charging forward. One of them was able to head the ball into the net between their player at the near post and the scrambling goalkeeper into the net. GOOOAL! As one of their defenders tossed the ball out of the back of the net, I heard the stunning sound of three whistles. The game was over! We had won!

So Julie asked, "How did the Fusion players react?"

"Some of them were pretty sore, but many of them at least shook hands. Their goalkeeper offered to swap jerseys with me, a definite act of sportsmanship. I had to give him another one because I suspected that my game jersey would be a museum piece somewhere. He understood that. As a footballer I am honored to have his Fusion jersey. I'm sure he would not wear that one again in any case."

"What happened to Penzeance after that?"

"We actually won the next round too, but in the fifth round we drew Arsenal, a great North London side. They had heard about our upset before and were loaded for bear. They brought almost all of their heavy artillery and crushed us 8-0, which is what would reasonably have been expected with the Fusion."

"Now let me get back to David and Goliath and why that was so important. Goliath represented the idea that "might makes right." He was huge. He worshiped a god of human creation. What restraint was there with him? David joined faith and intellect. He worshiped the Creator; instead of human beings creating a god as in the case of Goliath and later described in Isaiah 44, David acknowledged that he had been created by the invisible God and worshiped Him. Although David did not always follow through, he acknowledged the importance of obeying God's commands and serving Him. Psalms 19, 100 and 119 are representative examples. David realized that human might did not always make right. Instead of trusting himself, David trusted God and even prophesied of the future great Messiah, Who combined man and God in one. Psalms 22 through 24, 2, 45 and 69 are some examples. If David had died as a teenager in battle against Goliath, all of these precious truths might not have been known. Although God had myriad other choices, David was the one that He used to shape history.

When David committed his great sin with Uriah and Bathsheba, God used David to teach us so much about the forgiveness of God. God had every right to kill David outright, but He did not. The result of this is recorded in Psalms 38, 51 and 32 as well as other places. David is a forerunner of everyone who has had to recover from slavery to sin of any kind.

In turn, David raised Solomon, who is often considered to have been the wisest man short of Jesus Christ to have ever walked the earth. Of all possibilities, God chose Bathsheba to be Solomon's mother notwithstanding the awful sin with which this relationship started. At the very opening of Proverbs (1:8), Solomon tells us to remember the teaching of both father and mother. In that time period, such mention of a female is unusual. Solomon's wisdom in Proverbs and Ecclesiastes and his insight into the relationship between male and female and the future relationship of Jesus Christ and His Bride, the Church, all hinged on David's survival and victory in his first battle with Goliath.

David's wars welded Israel into a nation and provided Solomon with a generation of peace which paved the way for Solomon to build the Temple that David had planned and designed. The tremendous prosperity of Israel under Solomon was based in part on the security of the borders won by David. Further Psalms were written for the new Temple worship. All of this was under the plan of God to pave the way for His Son to come to earth, but nevertheless God chose to use a few extraordinary people to influence the entire human race."

"There is another lesson from David and Goliath. Sometimes the fresh faith of youth that seems so naïve is actually a powerhouse under the hand of God. David was too young to 'know' that he could not fight Goliath. In fact David never intended to be close enough to risk Goliath's weapons but to strike at a distance with his slingshot. People can be so conditioned by their experience that they think that God cannot accomplish the impossible. King Saul had no answer for Goliath despite his battle experience. David acted in faith and courage forged in God's deliverance from wild animals. Our Penzeance team may have been so green that we did not know that it was impossible for us to defeat Man Fusion. As the Scriptures say, '*All things are possible to him who believes.*' Mark 9:23." (compare also Matthew 19:26, Mark 10:27 and Luke18:27)

Julie asked Sandy, "As a culture we are disregarding all this. In Scotland as late as perhaps 1940 or 1950 these things were considered important by many. Now we think it's irrelevant. What do you predict the result to be?"

Sandy first disclaimed any precise knowledge of the future. "When Jesus Christ returned to heaven from which He came, He told His disciples that 'It is not for you to know the times or the seasons.' Neither do I. But from the Scriptures I do know the general course of events. Our Lord Jesus in Matthew 24 and Paul in 2 Thessalonians 2 both warned of a massive apostasy that would be one of the signals that the end of human history as we know it is near. It looks like the groundwork for that apostasy is being laid. With the withdrawal of the influence of Jesus Christ and of the Holy Spirit whom His Father sent in His place, humanity will revert to barbarism and the Devil Incarnate, the Anti-Christ, will rise to power for what I understand to be just short of 7 years. If we consider the worst period of Nazi misrule to start with the *Krystalnacht* in November 1938 with its end in May 1945, we might have a good preview of what this might look like. If I understand Revelation correctly, half the earth's population will die and conditions would deteriorate to the point where the human race would make itself extinct if Jesus Christ did not return to earth and stop the carnage by throwing the Anti-Christ directly into the Lake of Fire, the ultimate place of the damned. The general direction appears to be clear enough, although the timing is not."

Julie then asked, "Then what hope do we have?"

Sandy responded, "On earth, none in the end. But this earth is not the end of the story. Our Lord Jesus said in John 14:1-3, '*In my Father's house there are many mansions. If it were not so, I would have told you. I go to prepare a place for you. And if I go I will come again, that where I am you may be also.*' God has been most merciful to me. I know that He is taking me to Himself. This implies the resurrection of the dead. The Lord Jesus demonstrated that resurrection in His own body after the most horrific death imaginable. He said to Martha, *'I am the Resurrection and the Life. He that believes in Me, though he were dead, yet shall he live. And whoever believes in Me shall never die. Do you believe this?'* (John 11:25-6) That same day Jesus Christ proceeded to demonstrate what He said by raising Lazarus from the dead after his corpse had been in a tomb for 4 days—so long that stench and decay had begun to set in. After discussing Noah's Flood and the coming destruction of this world by fire, Peter said, [2 Peter 3:13] *'Nevertheless, according to His promise, we look for a new heavens and a new earth in which righteousness dwells.'* That is where our hope is, and it is a sure and steadfast one. I claim no righteousness of my own because I have none. But I have been given and retain the righteousness God has given me through the blood of the Lord Jesus Christ sacrificed for my sin and then raised from the dead to pray for me continuously [Romans 8:34]."

Julie realized that she had found the answer she had been seeking. Sandy was genuinely different from the many wimps and phonies with whom she was acquainted. His talks were no act but came from the heart of a genuine man. But she had unexpectedly found more than that. She had heard the Gospel from Sandy and realized that it alone could satisfy her heart and soul. She craved hope; Jesus Christ and the Holy Spirit gave it to her. And finally she believed that she had found a man short of Jesus Christ that she could trust and who would be good for her and to her. Sandy's faith and masculinity touched her deep within her soul. The prospect of her living with him for the rest of her life seemed delightful while the prospect of living alone with her father or with someone else seemed pale and washed-out by comparison. But would Sandy agree? Julia dared not say this directly to Sandy but she breathed a short prayer to God asking for Sandy as her husband if it was His will.

At this point Sandy and Julie both had to leave. She wanted to see her father and had classes in the morning. Sandy had a clinic in the morning for prospective professional goalkeepers followed by team practice in the afternoon. Both had a full day ahead, so they verified their e-mails and cell phones and left matters there for the moment.

Part 1

Chapter 8

A fortnight later, Sandy arrived promptly after dinner at 7:00 Friday night at Julie's house. Both Julie and her father were there, with the sitting room of the house neat and tidy. Sandy was clean and dressed his best. After preliminary greetings everyone sat down to talk. Sandy expressed his condolences on Mrs. Kerr's death, and Mr. Kerr thanked him. Basically, Julie listened and observed as two strong-willed men appraised each other. This exchange occurred at Mr. Kerr's home ground.

Father: Julie tells me that you used to play football. How far did you go?

Sandy: I played goalie on the famous—or infamous in Manchester—Penzeance side in one of the biggest shock results ever in the English FA Cup. I thought I could have gone farther than League One, but I received some eminent advice that I was better at teaching youth how to play football than I was as a goalie myself. So I shifted to holding youth clinics in England and America teaching football and the Gospel in the evenings. I have been doing that for the past 2 years or so.

Father: What kind of structure do you have to protect yourself in case a young men is injured during one of your clinics?

Sandy: I thank the Lord that nothing like that has happened. When I go to America, there is a company that handles setting up the fields and equipment that I suppose has insurance. I never thought about that in England. The National Health Insurance in England would take care of the medical treatment if something happened here.

Father: But does that deal with major, long-lasting injury?

Sandy: I have never considered that from a legal point of view. I would gather that you are recommending that I have insurance to cover any liability.

Father: Do you earn enough to support a family?

Sandy: Modestly, yes. I am not wealthy. I should observe that the tax code makes the accumulation of wealth rather slow and difficult if one starts off without it.

Father: But what if I think that Julie is worth a lot more than a modest living?

Sandy: We are not engaged now. If and when that situation may arise with me or with anyone else, that is something that Julie would have to decide for herself. If I propose, I will be sure that Julie knows my finances thoroughly.

Father: What business training do you have, if any?

Sandy: I have no education directed specifically at running a business. I do have the practical experience of administering my clinics and paying the bills as they come due.

Father: Have you had any training in accounting?

Sandy: No, sir.

Father: What are your revenue sources?

Sandy: We do charge fees for young men to come to the clinics and we also can sell football jerseys and equipment for revenue. Since the Gospel is a component of my clinics, certain generous interested parties supplement the revenue from the football instruction.

Father: Is your soccer-related revenue rising or falling, and by how much on an annual basis?

Sandy: Revenue has been rising by about 8% annually.

Father: But are you not limited by your own ability to cover events? What if you have requests for 2 clinics during the same time period? What provision have you made for expansion if you should be successful?

Sandy: This is an excellent question. I would have to find another like-minded person with both the love of the Gospel and football training skills. Such people are not easy to find. So far I have been able to juggle requests so that I have not had to issue a refusal.

Father: Then I would suppose that your clinic business supports you but does not go much farther than that. Do your relatives have major assets?

Sandy: Nothing of which I am aware. That is not something we discuss.

Father: Do any of them own a Bentley, a Rolls Royce or a Mercedes?

Sandy: No.

Father: How old is your car?

Sandy: Nearly 8 years old, sir.

Father: Do you own a house?

Sandy: No. At this point the property taxes are prohibitive.

Father: Do you have any work experience outside of football?

Sandy: No.

Father: What are you going to do when your body wears out enough that you cannot keep up the clinics?

Sandy: So long as God continues to grant me health, that time is a good way off. There are football coaches who are in their sixties and seventies. I have already considered this when I switched from playing to clinics. I can instruct far longer than I could play if we make normal assumptions. But God sometimes surprises us with unexpected opportunities too.

At this point Julie offered to bring out dessert, and both Mr. Kerr and Sandy accepted. After some small talk, Mr. Kerr politely indicated that Sandy should give him time to talk with Julie. Their eyes met and they nodded to each other. Sandy had a game to coach the next morning in any case, so leaving was convenient for him also.

Mr. Kerr then spoke to his daughter. "This young man is courteous, well spoken and reasonably intelligent, but what else does he bring to the table? He has no money and little earning power. I couldn't hire him now at the company without extensive training of some kind if I wanted to do so. There is no way that he is ready to marry a young woman like you.

Julie answered, "As he said, we are not engaged. I think enough of him to arrange an introduction and am glad we are discussing the subject. You asked me what he brings to the table. He brings character. He is no wimp. He certainly did not show fear in the face of your searching inquiry. I have observed too many women who are miserable because they see their boyfriends or husbands—and I will have a husband and nothing less—fold up like a cardboard box under the least amount of pressure. You have taught me by your example that a good man at home is strong rather than fearful."

Father: If you want to marry after you graduate, let me look for a suitable man that is not a wimp but has some real money behind him. There are times when you will really need it, and it is always more enjoyable to live with money than without it.

Julie: You and I are looking at different things in a man. How can you select for me?

Father: I have more experience and know more about life than you do.

Julie: In terms of business, you're right. But you don't know me as well as I know myself.

Father: Are you really in a rush to marry? You're only 21 years old. Aren't we talking about something several years off, when you will know much more than you do now?

Julie: And what am I to do in the meantime? I will have my degree in biology, but I would need much more education in that field to make a good living there. Teaching is a possibility, but not an appealing one. Besides, I would still be alone. We both know how hard that can be.

Father: Would you want to work for me in the company? That would give you a place to wait.

Julie: You know that being the boss' daughter would be an extraordinarily difficult situation. And just as with Sandy, I too would need training before I would be competent to work for the company even with the degree. You know that you would be hiring me because I am your daughter and not because I am qualified for a position. That's not fair to anyone. There might even be the risk that I would make an error and cause a rift between us or between you and a key employee.

Father: You make good points there, but nevertheless you seem to be in a terrible hurry. Why did you want Sandy to meet me? Certainly not to pay tiddlywinks!

Julie: Sandy is the first man that has interested me, and not because he started off trying to do so. I have heard a few of his talks. His views are based on the Bible and are so different from anything I hear at the university that I decided to see if he is a fake. If he is, I can't find the evidence. Of course he is not perfect but everything I see indicates that he is genuine. "What you see is what you get." He is really a masculine man, which is so unusual these days. That's as far as matters have gone so far, but I would be pleased if he wants to marry me. I would be terribly shocked and disappointed if he wanted relations with me without marriage first. I don't think he is that kind of man. I know so little about love for God but I do think that a man who loves God is more likely to love his wife too.

Father: Julie, take your time. I understand that he has not proposed to you yet, but you seem to be so eager for a lifetime commitment. Your friends probably will not marry until about age 28. Why not wait with them?

Julie did not answer her father, but in her mind she realized that asking Sandy—if he ever screws up the courage to ask her after tonight's encounter—to wait until he is nearly 35 is out of the question. She remembered Shakespeare's poetic line: "There is a tide in the affairs of men, taken at the flood, leads on to fortune." Julie reflected that her flood tide might be very near.

Upon this they both went to bed.

In the meantime Sandy went to his flat and prayed, seeking an assurance from God. He believed that he loved Julie and would be content with her as his wife, but God is the best matchmaker. The conventional counsel concerning marriage seems to be always to wait, but for what? There can always be an excuse for delay. Sandy was 27, amply mature to know his own mind. But Sandy wanted the mind of God, and as he prayed he believed he knew to go ahead and propose. Sandy remembered that Jacob was attached to Rachel faster than he had become attached to Julie. The seven years' delay in Jacob's case made no difference in his feelings, but Jacob was so strong that he lived a life span about double those of today. Assuming that Julie professed faith in Jesus Christ, he saw no reason to wait. Sandy believed that Mr. Kerr had typical cold feet when a daughter was marrying but trusted that he would warm up in time. At least Mr. Kerr was forthright and truly cared for his daughter according to what he knew. His business questions were well thought out. Sandy was not intimidated by Mr. Kerr's challenges. He stayed up later than usual that night and had to focus himself on the next morning's game, but Sandy had in principle decided to propose marriage to Julie and that they marry fairly promptly after Julie's graduation. The next problem was to make arrangements to see Julie and to discuss it with her.

Sandy's team won a 3-2 cliffhanger the next morning. After he had dealt with all the post-game detail, he looked over his schedule and saw space Tuesday evening. Since Sandy did not want to call Julie's house, he sent an e-mail to Julie indicating that he wanted a private talk. Julie was relieved to hear from Sandy, having been concerned that her father may have put him off. So they made arrangements to meet at a more upscale restaurant than usual.

When they arrived, Julie asked Sandy what he thought of her father. Sandy answered that her father did care for her and had a good head for business. He certainly was intelligent. Sandy acknowledged that he was unlikely to satisfy her father's standards for earning money, but that he had a share in riches which Mr. Kerr did not understand. He pointed Julie to what Jesus had said at the well of Sychar in Samaria in John 4:32: *"I have food to eat of which you do not know."* He told Julie that there are riches greater than money, and that he would pursue those riches as a higher priority than British pounds. He then said this, "Who was richer, Peter and John or the rich young ruler? The rich young ruler left Jesus unhappy because he was clinging to his money when Jesus instructed him to give it up. (Luke 18:23) Peter and John went to the Temple one day and said to a beggar *'Silver and gold I have none, but what I have I give you. In the name of Jesus Christ of Nazareth, rise up, take up your bed and walk!'* (Acts 3:6) Julie, who was richer?"

Julie answered, "Peter and John ended up poor in money but rich in faith. They are famous even today. Do we know what finally happened to the rich young ruler? Do we even know him by name?"

"No," continued Sandy. "I do know from Hebrews 11:26 that Moses thought that even the reproaches of Christ were riches, in fact greater riches than in the richest country of his time.

"From our one meeting I think that the difficulty with your father is that he can see the uses of earthly money but has no conception of heavenly riches. I pray that this will change.

Perhaps he will talk with me about that. I pray that he will come to know and value the riches of God in Christ Jesus."

Sandy continued, "Now I have a question for you. What do you think of my Father?"

Julie said, "I have never met your father and do not even know if he is still alive."

Sandy said, "My human parents are both dead. I apologize. I was too cryptic. What do you think of my Father in heaven?"

Julie responded, "From listening to you and then reading the Bible verses you mentioned I am convinced that God in heaven is the Creator of all things and of all people. More than that, I am persuaded that Jesus of Nazareth is the Son of God. I accept that He was born of the Virgin Mary and that He was crucified on the Cross and raised from the dead as the Scriptures say. I know so little of the Bible, but I am aware that it teaches that Jesus will judge at the Last Judgment. I believe that His blood and death has paid for my sin in full.

Sandy asked, "Do you say this because I teach it or do you believe this yourself?"

Julie answered, "Even if I were never to see you again for any reason I would still believe this."

Sandy said, "That's what I was praying to hear. I trust that you do not need to worry about not seeing me. If God allows my purposes to ripen fully, you and I will see each other almost every day. I believe that you are the one God has chosen for my wife and I want to marry you when convenient after your graduation sometime this fall. Here and now I am asking you to commit with me to marriage for the rest of our lives notwithstanding the reservations of your father."

Julie swallowed, blushed and smiled. "My answer is yes," she said firmly. "We will have to make many arrangements. Do you know a pastor to marry us? I do want my father to give me away at the wedding, but he does not have a regular church. We will have to do our best to have you get to know him better. He might appreciate you more. His major concern about you was money."

Sandy said, "I will arrange for a pastor, a church and a ring. I know almost nothing about large weddings and never thought of one for myself. What type of wedding would your father want? Within reason I am prepared to accommodate his views so long as the teachings of the Bible are observed. But I want us married in a church that honors the Holy Scriptures."

As Julie completed her studies, Sandy and she spoke to her father to make wedding arrangements. Mr. Kerr made his reluctance clear in courteous terms because Sandy had no appreciable earthly wealth. Sandy explained that he had enough and that his most pressing concern was not English pounds but treasure in heaven. "*Lay not up for yourselves treasure on earth, where moth and rust corrupt and thieves break through and steal. But lay up for yourselves treasures in heaven, where neither moth nor rust corrupt, nor do thieves break through and steal. For where your treasure is, there will your heart be also.*" Matthew 6:19-21. Julie with her usual optimism asked her father not to worry so much. While she was new to Christianity, she could understand the simplicity of God's promises to take care of His children. While not knowing it, Mr. Kerr had made this easier to grasp by taking good care of Julie as to monetary and earthly matters up to this time in her life. Mr. Kerr could appreciate that Sandy and Julie were relatively modest in their monetary desires for their wedding. Mr. Kerr wanted a somewhat more elaborate ceremony than they, to which they agreed. He also did promise to fund the reception and their honeymoon. Mr. Kerr was content that neither Sandy nor Julie wanted to be extravagent; what bothered him is that neither one had the wherewithal to be extravagent. For Sandy, money was useful but a secondary concern. For Mr. Kerr money was vital. At no time were voices raised or harsh words exchanged, but the canyon between Mr. Kerr's and Sandy's understanding of what real treasures are became clear.

QUESTIONS FOR REFLECTION & DISCUSSION

According to the story, what was Sandy seeking in a wife? What did he ascertain before proposing?

Did Julie start the story seeking a husband? What about Sandy attracted her?

Might you anticipate pitfalls from Julie's greater education compared to Sandy? If you were advising them prior to marriage, what suggestions would you make?

What do you think of Sandy's decisiveness?

Comment on the different standards which Julie and her father were using to assess prospective husbands.

Diogenes, a Greek philosopher, carried a lantern and said that he was looking for an honest man. Was Julie echoing his search? Was Julie on the right track in looking at Sandy's life to assess: a) his teaching, and b) his sincerity and honesty (the concepts are close in Greek)?

How important was it that Julie's convictions about Jesus Christ were independent of Sandy?

How do you define treasure? What is the most permanent treasure? How important is money as we live our life on earth? (Before you dismiss earthly money entirely, read Ecclesiastes 7:12.)

Part 1

Chapter 9

The wedding time had come. The groom had gotten through a high-scoring 4-3 win with his amateur soccer team earlier that afternoon. At least that kept him from fretting about what could go wrong and had served to keep him from seeing the bride before the wedding. In the meantime Julie spent the day getting ready for 17:00 hours, doing the countless things that brides do to make themselves look their best. There had been a strained feeling at the rehearsal and the rehearsal dinner the night before, but Julie put this down to the inherent stress of the occasion. At least she had slept well and had no worries about her groom doing something wild the night before. Sandy had scrambled home right after the game, had showered and then changed into his tux and driven to the church, arriving about 30 minutes before the appointed time as planned. He found a private place to pray briefly.

The bridesmaids and the ushers were there and the guests were taking their seats. Julie's father politely asked her one more time whether she wanted to go through with this. For him it was not too late to bail out—he would cover any financial repercussions from the cancellation. Mr. Kerr was still convinced that Sandy Thomas had no wealth (close to true in terms of human finance) and was not worthy of his daughter's hand. Neither would Sandy expand the family fortune for future generations; in this sense Mr. Kerr thought like the family in the movie *Titanic* who wanted to marry their young daughter to the dissolute scion of wealth to make sure of the family fortune and perhaps also to ensure their own retirement. Mr. Kerr himself had no plan to retire shortly since he was immersing himself in his work to mask his grief over the loss of his own wife. Julie repeated that she would go forward. She then went to the ladies' room for last-second freshening. Then Mr. Kerr decided that he would torpedo the wedding for his daughter's long-term welfare since he could not persuade her to withdraw. It would not serve his purpose just to leave and refuse to walk her down the aisle, so he joined his daughter just as if he were any other nervous father and walked her down the aisle.

The pastor saw father and daughter walking down the aisle right on time. As they arrived he opened with the familiar words of the traditional ceremony: "Dearly beloved, we are here in the sight of God . . . Who gives away this bride to be married?"

Mr. Kerr replied, "I refuse to give her away. The groom is not suited to my daughter's station of life and has no accomplishments worth mentioning. Julie is acting in haste in reaction to her mother's death, and she is leaving me in disregard to my own feelings and needs. This marriage should be canceled!" As he tugged on Julie's arm he continued, "Julie, come with me."

Julie jerked her arm away from her father and shouted, "No! Father, please control yourself and sit down." Sandy edged closer to the bride to be in position to get in between her and her father if he were to try to drag her away.

Mr. Kerr refused his daughter's request to sit down. He also said that he would not pay for the reception that had been planned after the wedding. "I am going now to cancel those arrangements, so don't bother going because the bills will not be paid. If you knew what was good for you, you would come with me."

Now the groom spoke up in the hearing of the whole congregation. "Julie needs no human father to give her away. This match is made in heaven. We on earth only obey and ratify what our Father in heaven has so graciously commanded for our blessing. Our Father in heaven gives her away, and I receive her from Him in faith."

The congregation was startled by these unexpected clashes in public. The pastor, sensing this mood and not knowing what else the father might attempt, skipped the planned preliminary symbols and proceeded directly to the heart of the matter. "Alexander Thomas, do you take Julie Kerr to be your lawfully wedded wife, to have and to hold from this day forward; for richer, for poorer; for better, for worse; in sickness and in health? Do you promise to forsake all others and hold exclusively to her until death do you part?"

The groom said firmly and loudly, "I do."

Then the pastor turned to Julie and repeated the time-honored words. "Julie Kerr, do you take Alexander Thomas to be your lawfully wedded husband, to have and to hold from this day forward; for richer, for poorer; for better, for worse; in sickness and in health? Do you promise to forsake all others and hold exclusively to him until death do you part?"

Julie said with intensity, "I do. Let all this congregation witness that I stand by my promise to marry this good man according to God's institution of marriage notwithstanding the disapproval of my father."

Then the pastor continued, "According to the authority vested from God as a shepherd of His flock and according to the human law of Scotland, I pronounce you Alexander Thomas and Julie Kerr Thomas man and wife. Sandy, you may kiss your bride." He did so with enthusiasm and gentleness. "I present to you Mr. and Mrs. Alexander Thomas!"

After the couple had reached the back of the church, Sandy turned and said to the guests, "I don't know what to do next, because it would not honor Christ to try to force our way into the reception hall when Mr. Kerr refuses to pay for it. So why not sing praises to God while we ask God what to do next?" So several psalms were sung.

Then the pastor said, "We have had a fitting wedding reception already, although far from the one that was planned." The best man checked on the get-away car and found that it was still intact with its contents, so no changes of clothes were needed. Sandy's apartment would do for the wedding chamber, because Mr. Kerr presumably would not pay for this either.

Before Sandy and Julie went to bed together for the first time, Julie said to him, "We should pray for my father." Sandy agreed and led in joint prayer. "O Father in heaven, we do pray for Julie's father, that you would forgive him for today. You know his heart; you know that he wants the best for Julie as he understands it. I would pray that you would enlighten his spiritual eyes and ears to perceive the truth about Jesus Christ and through that see that You Yourself have joined us in marriage to each other. We pray for reconciliation not only concerning this marriage but also between you and Mr. Kerr. We ask this through the blood of Jesus Christ shed for sinners and in His name." Sandy and Julie together said "Amen."

In the meantime, Mr. Kerr went back to his house and made notes of what he wanted to start on the following Monday. Some dealt with work items. One of the entries read, "Call the solicitor for appointment to review my will and trust." Another read, "Call Julie to arrange for her to remove her property from the house." A third read, "Review insurance policy beneficiary designations." But Mr. Kerr did not go to work Monday morning, which was unusual. At first his secretary thought it was perhaps some extra celebration of the marriage, but not after she heard of the unusual proceedings at the church. She called the house with no answer. As a precaution she asked a constable to check the property. He did so and found Mr. Kerr dead and cold in bed without apparent trauma. The coroner found that Mr. Kerr had had a massive heart attack, most probably in the small hours of Sunday morning, roughly 10-12 hours after the wedding. The constable tracked Julie through Sandy and informed her late Monday afternoon.

So within 48 hours Julie had taken a husband and lost her father. His funeral would have to be arranged. Julie faced this responsibility. It would not do to have the pastor who married them against her father's objection to conduct the funeral. Julie decided to see Mr. Kerr's secretary as the person still living who knew Mr. Kerr the best apart from herself. There was one silver lining to these events: Julie would be spared being in the middle of conflict between her father and her husband. But any children that God might give would have no grandparents.

So on Monday evening Sandy and Julie sat down to discuss the stunning turn of events. Julie thought that her father might have grown to like Sandy if he had had more time to get to know him. Mr. Kerr had always respected decisiveness, and Sandy was quick to shoulder responsibility and was more than willing to defend his opinions under pressure. But Sandy was not trained as a man of business and finance as was Mr. Kerr, and he had not gotten past that objection at the time of the marriage and of his death less than 12 hours later. Both men were competitive but in completely different spheres. Neither would back down from pressure. Julie reflected that her father had without knowing it by his example prepared her to marry a strong leader like Sandy and that this preparation was in the purpose of God.

So Sandy and Julie first tackled the funeral arrangements. Sandy also issued a public statement affirming their marriage but also regretting that he did not express forgiveness of Mr. Kerr at the wedding itself in addition to his determination to proceed with the marriage. Specifically, he said that, "It was only right to proceed with the marriage as Julie and I had so committed before God Himself. I do regret that I did not express forgiveness to Mr. Kerr on the spot. At the time I was focused on the marriage and anticipated being able to speak with Mr. Kerr with a purpose of resolving our disagreements after everyone had taken time to think. We now know that there was no time to wait. I can only pray as Stephen did (Acts

7:60) that God will not lay any possible sin against me to the charge of Mr. Kerr at the Judgment."

Then they consulted with the solicitors who had prepared Mr. Kerr's will and allied documents. They had not been modified for some time. As the only child Julie inherited her father's assets, although he may have intended to change them before his heart attack. Since he had not changed them before he died, the documents stood as written. They had provided for Mr. Kerr's wife, who had predeceased him, and then for Julie in the usual form.

Sandy noted that Mr. Kerr owned his shipping business and that neither one of them were either trained or suited to take his place. Sandy did not want either of them to divert the necessary time from their new marriage to discharge these duties permanently. As Sandy and Julie surveyed their choices, they saw their options as:

A) Sell the business to a competitor or consortium, perhaps using an investment banker to help;
B) Prepare the business for a public offering on a stock exchange, in which case a suitable CEO would have to be found quickly;
C) Dissolve the business. Sandy rejected this option because it would throw people out of work whose livelihoods depended on the business. Sandy did want a reliable income from the business capital but without tossing the other employees out of work. Julie agreed;
D) Retain ownership and find a suitable and honest professional manager to run the business. Neither Sandy nor Julie knew whether or not there was a suitable successor already working for the company and neither were at all sure how

> they could judge whether someone would be suitable or not. In this case the services of an executive search firm might be needed. As the owner Julie would be entitled to receive dividends from her privately held stock.

Sandy and Julie decided that they would serve God better by pursuing Sandy's ministry of the Gospel and using the income to ease the problem of support and funding. Julie would build on her training in biology by learning physical training and especially advanced first aid and physical therapy in case of injury on the pitch. In this way she could make some contribution to Sandy's work, and her cheerful disposition would be a good influence on someone in pain. It really made no sense for someone their age with no business experience to try to supervise the experienced executives at the company. So they decided to seek advice as to how to keep the business going until a more permanent ownership structure could be created, which might well take a year or more. Mr. Kerr's deputy would be the interim CEO. Depending on financial events, they would either sell the business whole or take it public. Sandy pointed out that the completion of the sale of the business would enable them to provide seed money for other ministries or to support the distribution of Holy Scriptures in places where they are not readily available. Instead of receiving for their ministry they could give to others and receive the blessing mentioned by the Lord Jesus, *"It is more blessed to give than to receive."* Acts 20:35.

QUESTIONS FOR REFLECTION & DISCUSSION

There is no simple Biblical answer to the problem of Julie becoming the owner of a business that she was not trained to run. What do you think of their solution?

What do you think of Mr. Kerr's attempt to derail the wedding and of Julie's defiance of her father?

If we were to continue this story, neither Sandy nor Julie would have in-laws. How might that affect the course of their marriage, both positively and negatively? What wisdom does this discussion give you as to your proper conduct if one of your children is married?

In the story Mr. Kerr died suddenly. Does any one of us know how long we will remain alive on this earth? If we were to change the story and have Mr. Kerr continue to live indefinitely after the wedding, how would you advise Mr. & Mrs. Thomas to relate to him?

Part 2

Reflections on 1 Corinthians 7

One of the most neglected Scriptures in the Bible is 1 Corinthians 7. It contains practical answers to many issues about marriage. As background, the Lord Jesus had settled the basic question of what constitutes a proper reason for divorce in Matthew 19:1-12 (taking the most comprehensive statement). Physical sexual impurity is the only reason He allowed. But Jesus Christ lived in Israel and was questioned by Jews. The Apostle Paul in Corinth was dealing with a church with both Jewish and Gentile members in a culture that was Greek and far apart from that of Israel. Within Greece, Corinth was a particularly immoral city in Biblical terms, perhaps like the modern San Francisco in this respect. The prevalence of immorality in Corinth shows up in 1 Corinthians 5 & 6. So issues arose in Corinth that had no resemblance to family life in Israel. Through the Holy Spirit Paul gives expanded instruction to cover these newly encountered issues. The Corinthian church did not know how to deal with such questions and asked Paul, as noted in 1 Corinthians 7:1.

Before proceeding with 1 Corinthians 7, the seriousness of physical union between man and woman in 1 Corinthians 6:13-20 should be understood, as modern culture ignores this truth. Paul uses the expression "one flesh" to apply to any instance of sexual intercourse. This is the same expression as is used of the marriage of Adam and Eve. Properly speaking, marriage and sexual intercourse are automatically joined together except in cases of adultery and rape, which were capital crimes in the Old Testament. Under Moses' Law, an instance without force of sexual intercourse between two unmarried people of itself resulted in their marriage to each other. Deuteronomy 22:28-29. In this case no divorce was permitted for any cause. Paul's teaching in 1 Corinthians 7 should be understood against the background of settled doctrine that sexual intercourse between an unmarried man and an unmarried woman results in automatic marriage. There is absolutely no room for any form of temporary sexual union, whether in the form of a modern "hook-up", in the form of prostitution, in the form of temporary marriages practiced by some Shia Muslims in Iran or in any other guise that human imagination may devise.

In common with the Lord Jesus in Matthew 19, Paul prized the genuine gift of celibacy. The Lord Jesus warned that celibacy was not for everyone (Matthew 19:11-12). Paul similarly recognized that celibacy is not for all (1 Corinthians 7:6-9). One of the great tragedies of religious history has been and remains the efforts of various religions to enforce celibacy upon people who have not been given the gift of God to be celibate. Paul's warning that *"it is better to marry than to burn"* echoes through centuries of scandal both within and outside churches. Celibacy is a prized gift but rare. In fact, the rarity of celibacy has been necessary for the survival of the human race.

Paul also settles the issue of polygamy by forbidding it in 1 Corinthians 7:2. Note the singulars here: *"Let each man have his own wife, and let each woman have her own husband."* Each has one exclusive partner. This is an alteration of the Law of Moses, which on its face had allowed polygamy under strictly controlled conditions. Paul brought marriage back to its original foundation of one man married to one woman that is found in the Creation. This again is the same approach that Jesus Christ took in Matthew 19:8, *"Moses because of the hardness of your hearts permitted you to divorce your wives, but from the beginning it was not so."* Then the Lord Jesus forbade divorce except for sexual immorality. The foundation of the doctrine of marriage is the Creation.

Paul also discusses the physical aspects of marriage in 1 Corinthians 7:3-5. Although Paul himself was single, he shows here an understanding of the most intimate aspects of marriage. Some theorize that Paul had once been married, also based on his one-time membership in the Sanhedrin. I disagree based on Paul's own statements of his personal history. I will by-pass detailed discussion except that I believe that traditional Jewish instruction of young men would have given Paul enough knowledge that he would have comprehended what the Holy Spirit was instructing him in this passage. Paul makes it clear that married Christians are both spiritual and physical people and that both sets of proper desires must be met within the marriage. In verse 5, Paul specifically warns against prolonged postponement of intimate marital relations even for high and holy spiritual purposes. Extended postponement opens the door for Satanic temptation. In verse 4 Paul gives a basic principle that husband and wife should share their bodies with one another when either partner desires the intimacy. Married Christians do not own their own bodies; each partner owns the body of the other. In computer terms, the "default setting" should that the marriage partners will enjoy one another, and refraining from this God-given enjoyment should be the exception rather than the rule. Nature will tell us that frequency will gradually decline as the partners age and may eventually cease if and when one partner becomes and remains physically unable to join with the other, but regular and satisfyingly frequent marital intimacy as the parties are able and as either party desires it is a core, essential element of Christian marriage so long as both parties are capable physically.

This principle is the counterpart of marital exclusivity underlying the prohibition of adultery in the Seventh Commandment. Proverbs 5:15 commands, "*Drink waters out of your own cistern and running waters out of your own well.*" As one reads on in Proverbs 5, there can be no doubt that the Holy Spirit through Solomon is speaking of marital sexual intercourse. We understand physically that even on a day of physical labor under a scorching sun that enough water will satisfy thirst. This Scripture is applying this truth to intimacy within marriage. It is vital to keep returning to one's own well and to partake from no other (Proverbs 5:17). Since Solomon's instructions are in the first instance to his son, this is expressed in male terms; this makes perfect sense because we know that the average male is more prone to stray from his exclusive mate than the average female. He is to "*rejoice with the wife of his youth*" (Proverbs 5:18) and to "*be always ravished with her love.*" (Proverbs 5:19). The references to a wife's breasts in Proverbs 5:19 removes any doubt that the Holy Spirit is speaking of physical love between husband and wife. God regards physical marital attraction and love as holy and as one of His precious gifts to the human race. Leaving aside exceptions for physical inability, marital sexual intercourse is as essential for the married person as water is to the laborer. In both cases one should drink copiously enough to fully satisfy one's thirst.

So what if you are married and physically able but don't feel the intimacy with your mate and have no desire for marital intimacy? Please, stop and pray! Both you and your marriage partner are in serious trouble for this reason alone. If that does not restore your desire for intimacy with one another, then Nike with its slogan for athletic training has the right idea to start your restoration. Resume your intimacy with your marriage partner just because it is right even if you don't feel like it in the beginning. Trust God that He will restore your enjoyment as you start to obey again.

Starting in 1 Corinthians 7:10, Paul repeats the basic instruction of the Lord Jesus forbidding divorce. Paul does not even mention adultery, which had already been settled by the Lord Jesus. But in verse 12, Paul explains that he is now addressing matters on which Jesus Christ had never spoken. *"But to the rest I speak, not the Lord."* Paul is not disclaiming apostolic authority from the Holy Spirit but pointing out that he is now going beyond the specifics of what the Lord Jesus had taught while on earth. The first issue he mentions is the matter of a marriage between a believer and an unbeliever.

How could this have become a practical issue? Consider Paul's preaching in Corinth. From Acts 18:1-17, we know that both Jews and Gentiles were saved. It is highly probable that in some cases one partner of a pre-existing marriage was saved and the other was resistant to the Gospel. In some of these cases the resistant partner still wanted to live with his or her spouse, and in other cases the resistant spouse was so averse to the Lord Jesus that he or she wanted nothing to do with the transformed partner and bolted the marital home or expelled the Christian. Each of these situations posed a specific issue not mentioned by the Lord Jesus on earth:

1. If the unbelieving spouse bolts and will not resume living as in marriage, is the believer still bound to the marriage?
2. If the unbelieving spouse wants to stay, how should the believer react? Is there any ceremonial uncleanness with the unbeliever or with the offspring of a believer and an unbeliever? (This set of questions might resonate especially with people of a Jewish background.)
3. Should the believer break up the marriage because of the spouse's unbelief?

The last question is the easiest to answer. The simple answer is no, found in 1 Corinthians 7:12-13. It should not be the believer that insists upon the break-up of the marriage because of the spouse's unbelief. This rule remains the same regardless of whether it is the man or the woman who has faith. Given that premise, the issues in the second question must be faced. Some might object that an unbelieving spouse is unholy in a ceremonial sense and that therefore the believing spouse should not touch them. In Leviticus, a person ceremonially clean becomes unclean by touching a leper, a corpse or other contaminated object. But Jesus Christ reversed this: whenever He touched a leper, the unclean became clean. This new principle applies in marriage so far as any issue of ceremonial uncleanness is concerned. Christ has touched and healed spiritually one party to the marriage. Then the entire household is now clean for this purpose, including husband and children who are not yet saved. The converted spouse should afford and enjoy all appropriate family relations that are appropriate in each case while praying for the conversion of the other members of the household.

That returns us to the first question as to what happens to a marriage when the unbelieving party refuses to remain after the conversion of one spouse. At this point in the epistle, Paul is dealing with a subject that the Lord Jesus Himself did not address on earth (1 Corinthians 7:12) Paul's answer in 1 Corinthians 7:15 is clear. In this situation the believer is not bound to the old marriage when the unbelieving marriage partner absconds from the marriage. This raises one further question: if the believer is set free from the old marriage, does the abandoned believer have liberty to enter a new one?

A straightforward reading of 1 Corinthians 7:15 and the following verses appears to say that an abandoned believer is free from the old marriage so as to be able to enter a new one without sinning against God. "*A brother or sister is not in bondage in such cases, but God has called us to peace.*" The word translated "bondage" is the usual one for slavery and is found later in 1 Corinthians 7 and translated "servant" in the King James version. It often means an outright slave who can never on his or her own leave his or her master's service. For the Christian whose spouse refuses to remain without his or her driving the spouse away, the meaning is that the remaining Christian is not bound to the departed spouse any more than in Romans 7:1-4 a Christian would be bound to a deceased spouse. This reading is confirmed in 1 Corinthians 7:27-28: "*Are you bound to a wife? Do not seek to be loosed. Are you loosed from a wife? Do not seek a wife. But if you marry, you have not sinned, and if a virgin marries, she has not sinned.*" Some translators are unwilling to translate these words at face value. I have seen versions of the Bible that alter "Are you loosed from a wife?" to "Are you unmarried?" This would be a completely different Greek word if "unmarried" were meant. The word in 1 Corinthians 7:27 for "bound" is the same as in Romans 7:2, also dealing with marriage. Paul, as a trained lawyer, was precise in his language and we dare not take the freedom to alter it. This is even more true when we reflect that the ultimate author of the Scriptures is the Holy Spirit. There are different words for "loosed" in Romans 7 and in 1 Corinthians 7 that reflect the different causes of the dissolution of the marriage: death v. departure. But the end result is the same. The first marriage is destroyed and the believer is left with the liberty to live singly if one can or to remarry if that is better for the particular person. 1 Corinthians 7:27, speaking specifically to people loosed from a wife, makes it clear that such people may remarry notwithstanding the potential dangers of marriage that Paul will discuss later. Similarly (v. 28), virgins may marry. (Bear in mind that Paul has also spoken vividly in 1 Corinthians 7:10 of the dangers of being single.) Given the earlier principles in this chapter in which men and women are treated as having equal rights, those principles should be extended here too. Paul is using the man as an example rather than speaking of men only and not women (see 1 Corinthians 7:12-15 and especially verse 15 referring to both believing men and believing women to remove any doubt on this score). Clearly the same result would apply if a Christian's marriage were to be destroyed through physical adultery by an unfaithful spouse of either sex, as indicated by the Lord Jesus in Matthew 19:1-12. No human being nor combination of human beings has any authority to alter these principles for Christians in Scripture, which come from the Lord Jesus and the Holy Spirit, either to make them more stringent or more permissive.

The Holy Spirit through the Apostle Paul introduced a concept which has been of great practical benefit to both the Christian Church and to the whole world when He mentions "calling" in 1 Corinthians 7:20. While the term in the epistle is flexible and can apply to being married or single, being circumcised or uncircumcised, to being free or slave, or to occupation, its impact as an occupation has been immense. Especially in countries strongly influenced by the Reformation, one's calling in terms of earning a living could be as holy and as useful to God as a calling into the ministry. Max Weber, an early sociologist, thought the concept of a personal calling in terms of occupation fueled the Industrial Revolution and Europe's economic expansion during the 19th century. In this concept, an occupation or trade is not merely a means of earning a living or investment money. An occupation is also a trust from God to serve Him within the community. At any given time, a coal miner, an accountant or a business owner may be a focus of God's plan to bring blessing to a community. The deliverance of Naaman from physical leprosy and from the sin which was symbolized by that leprosy began with a word from a young servant girl of Israel who had been seized as a captive. 2 Kings 5:3-4. She may have been a kitchen worker or a seamstress. God does not confine His dealings with people to the four walls of a sanctuary. He may intervene to provide for and even prosper an individual believer for His good purposes, which may be revealed only later. To take an example from Genesis, only through the Bible can we see that God's provision for Hagar in Genesis 21:14-21 was the beginning of the rise of the Arab people. One example of God's direct preservation of the people of Israel is found in 2 Kings 6:8-7:20. In terms of modern society, Christians should regard their work as an extension of God's witness to the world.

In terms of religious history, one thinks of the time after the American Civil War to the end of the 19th century as the age of Moody and Spurgeon. Indeed these men were called of God to His ministry and were greatly used. But in the realm of business J.C. Penney, William Colgate and John Wanamaker were prominent Christians in the American business world; there were counterparts in Great Britain as well. Moving forward in time to World War 2, General George Patton, as profane as he could be in his moments of anger, had a sense of calling from God and destiny as a soldier that kept him going after his worst failures. General MacArthur also had a sense of divine mission and destiny. Admiral Ramsey of the Royal Navy believed that the help of God was essential to D-Day and that his forces would receive it. After World War 2 came Billy Graham as an evangelist. The power of faith in carrying out a God-given task, small or large, has been demonstrated millions of times over. Whatever your calling may be (unless you are claiming a calling forbidden by God), if it is from God and if you are willing to dedicate it and yourself to God, He will use it for good and for righteousness.

Conversion to Christianity does not necessarily mean an immediate change of calling. In 1 Corinthians 7:20 the Apostle Paul lays down the basic principle: "*Let every man abide in the same calling in which he was called.*" Once more Paul is using men as illustrative of male and female. This matches the principle in the earlier verses that new Christians were not to leave old marriages but rather live within those marriages as Christians if possible. As applied to status, a person saved while legally free should remain free, while a person saved while enslaved to a human master should continue to accept that status if freedom were to be unavailable and practice his Christianity within the constraints of slavery. Freedom is to be taken if available. These principles are found in 1 Corinthians 7:21-24.

Conversion changes the inner man first, while resulting changes to the outer man come later. So it proved for Onesiphorus, who was saved as a runaway slave through Paul's preaching and was sent back to his master Philemon along with Paul's request for Onesiphorus' legal liberty for the sake of the Gospel. This request is the Epistle to Philemon. Since Philemon owed Paul far more than Onesiphorus' merchandise value because Paul had brought the gospel to Philemon (we simply do not know about any financial transactions), Paul anticipated that his request to Philemon would be granted and Philemon's debt to Paul would be reduced accordingly. Paul definitely wanted Philemon free, but he did respect the legal system in which he lived by sending Onesiphorus back to Philemon first. For Onesiphorus, the first changes were in his heart and mind; the legal changes followed later. This is the sequence likewise presented in the great Old Testament prophecies of the New Covenant: Jeremiah 30-33 and Ezekiel 36:24ff.

Based on these principles, one might inquire about the righteousness of the American Civil War. The fact that Christians in Paul's time were commanded to tolerate their slave status (unlike the slaves of the rebellion led by Spartacus over 100 years earlier, which probably would have substituted one set of masters for another had it succeeded) does not make slavery right. Permanent slavery within Israel (longer than 7 years) was impossible under the Law of Moses without the consent of the person restricted. Given the prevalent ignorance of the day in which Paul lived, one questions whether a better system was then workable that would still preserve order that makes freedom possible. Haiti abolished slavery by revolution but was unable to establish freedom. We should remember that it was the 18th and 19th centuries before national political systems developed which could function without slavery or without its cousins serfdom or a caste or class system. By 1860, the United States did have experience in slaveless systems in Northern states. In both North and South, there was substantial respect for the Bible. So there was a foundation for the abolition of slavery in the United States (which the Christian statesman Wilberforce had already accomplished in Great Britain through God's power) that was lacking in the Roman Empire of Paul's time.

But in fact American slaves did not engage in mass uprisings by force in 1859 as John Brown hoped. Nat Turner had led a small rebellion earlier, but John Brown did not attract any rebellious slaves at Harper's Ferry. In fact, it was the Southern states who rebelled against the electoral verdict of the 1860 election and attempted armed rebellion and secession. Several states had passed ordinances of secession before Abraham Lincoln had ever taken office on March 4, 1861. The abolition of slavery began as a military measure to destroy the fighting power of the rebellious South, as the history of the Emancipation Proclamation shows. As Northern armies swarmed through the South starting in 1863, slaves swarmed to the armies. It was the assertion of lawful national authority that led to the Thirteenth Amendment abolishing slavery. By early 1865 after Lincoln had been re-elected, abolition of slavery had become an aim in itself, but it is not accurate to read the consensus of 1865 into Lincoln's views in 1858 or 1860. Lincoln had gone no farther than opposing extension of slavery into United States territories that were not yet states. Abolition of slavery was a great blessing, but it was not achieved by any slave rebellion but rather as a blessed by-product of the preservation of the United States as one nation. Many Southern soldiers were individually righteous men. High-ranking examples are Generals Robert E. Lee, Stonewall Jackson and John Gordon.

But the cause for which they fought—the dissolution of the United States as a means of preserving slavery against the tide of history and against the teachings of Paul that all human beings are fundamentally equal (for example Acts 17:26, Galatians 3:26-29 and Ephesians 2:14-22)—was fundamentally wrong. I do not seek to cause offense, but in an American context some comment is necessary in order to understand that 1 Corinthians 7 is not putting God's approval on slavery merely because He tolerated that evil for that time and for centuries thereafter. In short, slavery in the Roman Empire was an evil but not justification for armed revolt.

A further point is that 1 Timothy 1:10 clearly condemns the slave trade, if not slavery directly. The King James translation uses "menstealers", but many translations use the term "slavetraders." This is in the context of an enumeration of sins forbidden by the Law of Moses. The Old Testament also forbids communities from returning runaway slaves. Deuteronomy 23:15. So it is wrong to say that the Bible approves slavery, even though God permitted its existence for centuries. Similarly, the Law of Moses made some provision for divorce (Deuteronomy 24:1-4) even though God hated it. Malachi 2:14-16.

There are instances in history in which God delays His correction and judgment for reasons we may not fully understand. Slavery in the Roman Empire was one such case.

Because the church in Corinth had converts from the Jewish synagogue and also Gentile converts of pagan background, Paul dealt with the issue of circumcision starting in 1 Corinthians 7:17. Amazingly, this issue has reappeared in modern San Francisco in the form of a proposed ordinance to forbid circumcisions of minors within that city, to the prejudice of

Jews who observe the Law of Moses and also of Christians who prefer to circumcise their male children on either medical or religious grounds. Muslims who follow Abraham's example in circumcising Ishmael would be equally prejudiced. A recent court decision in Germany has also raised this issue. In the ancient Roman Empire, Jews often considered uncircumcised people unclean and Gentiles often were equally prejudiced against Jews because of their circumcision. I would not be surprised if the rivalry between circumcised and uncircumcised was sometimes as intense as the rivalries among ethnic groups today. But Paul makes it clear that the entire issue has no significance for the Christian. The spiritual unity among Christians transcends any question of bodily appearance. There is no basis for pride before God. For other passages that expound this principle in greater detail, consult Romans 2 & 3, Galatians 2, 3 & 5:1-12 and Colossians 2.

Having discussed the questions of slavery and freedom and with circumcision versus uncircumcision, Paul then returns to being married or being single as a calling in verse 25. Two truths appear on the surface: (1) Some people serve God better being married, and others being single; and (2) One should not change one's current condition (whether married or single) without a definite reason to do so which is at least permitted in Scripture. One such reason has already been mentioned in verse 10—the inability to maintain self-control of sexual desires when single. The Lord Jesus likewise indicated in Matthew 19:11 that many people (especially but not exclusively adult men) cannot endure being single.

In verse 25 Paul makes clear that he has no general command from God for virgins. At this time, Paul's non-binding preference was for virgins and others who were single to remain single.

The first reason Paul gave was the "present distress." I do not know precisely what this was. Perhaps it was the famine that Agabus predicted as recorded in Acts 11:28. 1 Corinthians would have been written during the reign of Claudius, but we cannot be sure whether that famine had already occurred or whether it extended all the way from the Holy Land to Corinth. If not the famine, could the distress have been the attempted persecution recorded in Acts 18:12-17? Or was there a generalized economic depression that was not directly mentioned? Paul may have been anticipating general persecution which started within the Roman Empire about 10 to 15 years after Paul wrote this epistle. We do not know the specifics of the distress, but Paul thought it a reason for someone single to be wary of marriage for the short run. The second reason is that one acquires necessary earthly concerns when one marries. Within Biblical limits, one does need to please one's mate. If there are children, they bring special responsibility. All of these things limit one's time for direct worship of God and direct service to God. It is hard to imagine that Paul's ministry would have taken the form and extent that it did if Paul had been married. Imagine being Paul's wife when he endured all of the physical hardships mentioned in 2 Corinthians 11:23-28. Paul realized that not everyone could be like him, so he made no effort to direct that all unmarried believers remain unmarried. However, Paul does say that a single person who can bear singleness without spiritual trouble may have more potential than a married person for full-time service for Jesus Christ. This is summed up in 1 Corinthians 7:32-35.

Paul also warned in verses 29-31 that there is potential for sorrow through marriage. I do not think that Paul was here thinking of a mismatch within the relationship but rather the possibility of sorrow by reason of tragedy or trauma. His phrase *"the time is short"* hints at outside trouble to come. Indeed, in less than 20 years Paul was to be beheaded and Peter crucified upside down. The Bible does not tell us whether or not Peter's wife lived to witness her husband's death. We do know that Christian families have endured tragedy to loved ones throughout the history of the Christian church.

We have already written briefly about verses 27-28, but some further comment from a lawyer's perspective may help. We must let the words of Scripture speak without embellishment. *"Are you bound to a wife? Do not seek to be loosed. Are you loosed from a wife? Do not seek a wife. But and if you marry, you have not sinned. And if a virgin marries, she has not sinned."* I am aware that some translations substitute "are you unmarried" for "are you loosed from a wife." But this is taking unwarranted liberty with the Greek, in which Paul used the word "loosed" as the opposite of "bound." Verse 27 is not addressed to all unmarried people, but to those not married who had once been married. In context of the entire chapter, they may have become unmarried again by reason of either the death of their spouse or by the refusal of their spouse to live with them after their conversion. But the Greek unmistakably at this point is aimed at people who had been married but were no longer married as they read or heard Paul's epistle. This is reinforced by the fact that Paul specifically mentions virgins in verse 28 after his address to unmarried people who were not virgin in verse 27. Therefore, those truly freed from a spouse according to Paul's teaching and that of Jesus Christ (most fully expressed in Matthew 19:1-12) do not sin by remarrying. This is consistent with Paul's statement on widows in verses 39-40. His instruction there are similar: one is free to remarry but generally one will be happier to remain unmarried. As in Deuteronomy 24:1-4, a divorced person has the liberty to remarry despite the hazards involved. Similarly, in John 4 the Lord Jesus recognized 5 marriages for the woman at the well and carefully distinguished her current relationship as with a man not her husband.

As noted earlier, Paul's advice in verses 27-40 are not confined to either male or female. Paul uses the most likely cases as representative language comprehending all adult believers of either sex. In law we often have a catch-all clause in a document specifying that the entire document is to be read without regard to gender. I do not see that language in 1 Corinthians, but such language is found in Galatians 3:28. In terms of spiritual liberty, man and woman are equal in Christ Jesus, even though certain distinctions are preserved within marriage and within the church. The freedom to enter marriage or to refrain is the same for either sex.

The Bible as a whole and Paul in this epistle avoid any rigid rules as to whether an unmarried person should marry or remain unmarried. This passage and Matthew 19:1-12 do place a premium on singleness if this can be spiritually maintained. But the warning of both the Lord Jesus and of Paul in verse 10 indicate that many cannot do this and need to marry to maintain any sort of spiritual balance. Were it not so, the human race would not reproduce from generation to generation. In actual church history, most of the trouble is that too few people have married and remained married, rather than too many. To take but one historical example, much tragedy would have been averted if Abelard could have openly married Heloise. To return to the evil of slavery, much tragedy would have been averted if Thomas Jefferson would have openly married Sally Hemings after the death of his first wife. Extra-Biblical doctrines that have enforced singleness without regard for the special gift required to live single have paved the way for centuries of sexual tragedy involving both adults and children. It is not only the sins of individuals, but the very doctrine in contradiction of 1 Timothy 4:3 is at the root of these tragedies. Marriage is the norm for adult believers short of advanced age. This is reinforced the fact that the usual training ground for elders and deacons in the Christian church is the family, as expounded in 1 Timothy 3 and Titus 1. Moreover, Peter and the other original Apostles were married. 1 Corinthians 9:5. There is no basis to be more stringent than to require holiness within monogamous marriage for any church leader, although singleness is an option for those capable of living that way. But for most marriage is necessary and should be a blessing.

(For further consideration of issues raised in Parts 1 & 2, review Appendix B which contains in barebones form an actual example from real life late in the 20th century.)

Part 3

Human Marriage Superseded: Death and Judgment

In my first book *Warnings of a Watchman*, published by Trafford Press in 2010, I wrote briefly on the issues of same-sex relationships and of polygamy. I stand by what I wrote then but should comment further given the march of human sin since that time. Both polygamy and same-sex marriages have gained more acceptance since I first wrote. But is this a blessing or a curse?

When arguing before a judge in favor of marriage as being between one man and one woman, it is natural to base one's case on heterosexual monogamy working better, especially for children. But this is not the ultimate way moral questions must be decided. Since the Bible is God's Word, the Bible must be the final authority for what Christians believe. It is true that to avoid government oppression our political Founding Fathers forbade government establishment of any religion, but that does not mean that principles of right and wrong cannot be upheld just because they have religious roots. Otherwise, private property could not be protected because it too springs from the Bible. So does the law against murder. When we hear of legal and political arguments, we must remember that at best they spring from secondary sources of truth and not from the ultimate authority of the Scriptures.

In dealing with the definition of marriage, social science is finding that children as a whole do best with a committed father and mother staying in the same home throughout their years of growing up. You can check imapp.org and the research of Judith Wallerstein on the children of divorce for two places where these results are substantiated and for further references. So a "secular" justification of government recognition of marriage, an institution originated by God at the Creation, is the protection of children. Another reason is the need for a nation to replace its citizens as they age. Tumbling birth rates are apparent in the financial crises of Japan and of many nations in Europe where population decline is setting in, bringing into question a country's ability to care for its aged. Much of this is tied to declining marriage rates. Now that is being compounded by confusion as to what constitutes a marriage.

In modern society, many parents find themselves in less than an ideal situation, with two parents living apart from each other and the child dividing time between them. Or one parent may have disappeared completely or be confined in prison. Yet there is still hope in Jesus Christ for the remaining parent and the children, and even for an irresponsible parent who is willing to repent. Isaiah puts the most extreme case in Isaiah 49:15, "*Can a mother forget her nursing child, that she should not have compassion on the son of her womb? Yes, they may forget, but I [God] will not forget you."* Or consider Psalm 27:10: "*When my father and my mother forsake me, then the Lord will take me up.*" These are not empty promises. Look in Appendix B for a sketch of the life story of a person living today who is a living, walking testimony to the truth of these passages.

Genesis makes clear that the original marriage created by God between Adam and Eve was between one man and one woman. Divorce was permitted only in what ought to be exceptional cases of sexual impurity or refusal to live with the spouse. If the Bible is accepted as it should be, that is the end of the issue. But we know that large segments of society virtually everywhere in the world rebel against this. Unreconstructed Mormons (not a majority of modern Mormons, but a minority who seek to continue the practices of Joseph Smith and Brigham Young, including Warren Jeffs and Tom Green) and Muslims advocate polygamy. Many secular societies in effect practice serial marriage, swapping partners as one feels like it. This has infected the Christian church too. In many cases of serial marriage shorter affairs are interspersed. The late Pamela Harriman is an example of this lifestyle. Now there is a growing advocacy of same-sex marriage, with or without same-sex or bisexual relationships with others. Any of these choices represents a rejection of God and of His example in Creation.

We should remember that there is a constant war between God and Satan, as Satan continues his rebellion and tries to wrest control of Creation from God Himself. One of Satan's methods in his efforts to gain complete loyalty of the human race is to obscure the identity of God. To try to do that Satan attacks the family in order to blind people to the identity of God as

Father. If a child's image of a father is non-existant because of desertion, that is one way that Satan will work to that aim. This frequently happens when a birth is out of wedlock. If another child's father is abusive, that will distort God's identity as Father in a different way. Satan tries to deceive women into believing that there is no need for fathers in raising children. Or if Satan can scramble the family in a way that leaves the child with two fathers or no fathers, that is still a different method for Satan to advance his war objective of blinding people to God's love and care for them as Father. Depriving people of a sense of the fatherhood of God is one method for Satan to implant fear where faith should grow.

Conscious rejection of God's Word amounts to a declaration of war against Him. This may take the form of rejecting God's testimony concerning His Son Jesus Christ. God spoke from heaven several time concerning the fact that Jesus Christ was His Son. John 1:29-34, 12:28; Hebrews 2:3-4. Many in the United States have not forgotten the commotion when Congressman Joe Wilson called President Obama a liar during a Presidential address to Congress. Yet that is trivial compared to calling God a liar, whether about Creation, marriage or especially about His Son Jesus Christ. Nobody can continue to call God a liar and get away with it for long. If we call out to God, "You lie!", we bear the risk of having Him respond, "You die!" We should not forget that Ananias and Sapphira conspired to lie together to the Holy Spirit and that they both dropped dead on the spot (read Acts 5, also compare 2 Thessalonians 2:8, Psalm 139:19, Amos 9:4 and Revelation 19:19-21).

Drastic judgments have fallen historically on societies who have sinned against God by defying His commands concerning marriage and sexuality. We should remember that God may choose to be patient in this as in other matters, but there will be a reckoning sooner or later. God told Abraham concerning the Amorites that their iniquity was not yet full (Genesis 15:16) but that the men of Sodom were especially wicked (Genesis 13:13). Abraham and Lot lived to see the destruction of Sodom by fire, as recounted in Genesis 18-19. Just because Joseph Mengele escaped human justice for performing human experiments in Nazi camps does not mean that he has escaped divine justice. Quite the contrary. From everything we know Mengele never repented of his wicked acts and faces eternal punishment from an angry Creator. Jeremiah warned of God's judgment falling on a sexually licentious society in Jeremiah 5:7-9 and lived to see it happen. Even King David, one of God's true servants, lost 4 children and much peace for his sins of murder and adultery involving Uriah and Bathsheba. (See 2 Samuel, starting with chapter 11). God in His mercy spared David the ultimate punishment that his sins deserved, but that should not conceal the severity of God's chastisement. In many like cases God has exacted the full punishment instead of showing mercy.

Where does that leave contemporary society? In giving my opinion, I claim no special revelation from God. I am applying logic to the general revelation of God that we find in the Bible. I have no timetable, but as a human society we are in big trouble. To have some idea of how near the Last Days and the Last Judgment may be, we should consider several passages that are clearly connected to the end of the present age. One should be duly cautious in relying on one potential indicator alone because of our fallibility, but the combination of several indicators is reason to sound a warning, although we cannot have and never will have a precise timetable.

In Isaiah 11:10, the prophet through the Holy Spirit wrote of Jesus the Messiah as an ensign around which the Gentiles would rally. This has been in process of fulfillment since Peter witnessed to the house of Cornelius in Acts 10, although there were occasional instances of Gentile faith before that. In verse 11, we read, *"the Lord shall set His hand* ***the second time*** *(my emphasis) to recover the remnant of His people which shall be left from [various geographical locations from all points of the compass in relation to Israel]."* The first time occurred when after the fall of Babylon waves of exiles returned and organized under Zerubbabel and later under Ezra and Nehemiah. The second time is in progress as we speak, having started with the Zionist movement under Theodor Hertzl and furthered by Arthur Balfour, Chaim Weitzman and Winston Churchill starting in the late 19th century and continuing after World War 1. It has continued ever since, with the survivors of the Holocaust and the Jewish residents of the Middle East funneling into Israel after 1945, followed by many Russian Jews late in the 20th century. Jews have also returned from Africa and from the Western world. Though many of the people involved may not be conscious of this, they are returning to their ancestral home in fulfillment of divine prophecy. If one reads Isaiah 11 as a whole, it is plain that the subject is the Kingdom of the Messiah, which comes after the destruction of the Kingdom of Satan described in Revelation and elsewhere. The migrations of returning Jews are not only strengthening the current nation of Israel, they are also putting in place an ingredient for the return of Jesus the Messiah and His personal rule over Israel and over the entire world.

Ezekiel 38 is significant because it identifies a coalition that will oppose Israel in the Last Days. We cannot identify with precision Meshech and Tubal, but most expositors believe that they represent Russia. Turkey may also be a possibility. It is of note that both Russia and more recently Turkey are wary of Israel, even though the Soviet Union joined the United States in recognizing Israel in May 1948 and Turkey traditionally has been friendly with Israel. Persia is the modern Iran, which has not bothered to conceal its hostility to Israel since 1979. This followed a time of friendship between Israel and Iran under the Shah. Egypt had been an enemy of Israel from 1948 to 1979 and with the recent election of a Muslim Brotherhood candidate as President may revert to that enmity after over 30 years of peace. If so, this would mark a very dangerous time in which both Egypt and Iran would be simultaneous all-out enemies of Israel, which has not been true at least since 1954 when the Shah rose to power in Iran. Libya is now in the throes of establishing a new government, which may also turn out to be an enemy of Israel. If the Ethiopia of Ezekiel 38 is the same as the modern Ethiopia, this does not yet seem to be in place. If it refers to modern Somalia instead, that country is infested with pirates, is in anarchy and could try to turn on Israel on a dime. Once again, we have no timetable, but the pieces appear to be jelling for the coalition mentioned in Ezekiel 38. If Egypt and Iran join in an aggressive alliance, this would be highly dangerous for the Arabian peninsula and for Israel.

Interspersed through Matthew 24 are several indicators of the approach of the Last Days before the return of our Lord Jesus. To be thorough, one should also read and study Mark 13 and Luke 21, but the thrust of all three passages is largely the same. One of the questions within Matthew 24:3 is "*What [shall be] the sign of Your coming, and of the end of the world [or age]?* There are several answers in the remaining portion of Matthew 24. Yet Matthew 25 gives several parables indicating that many people will be blind to the signs and caught unawares. Some of the signs are:

A) False Messiahs (Matthew 24:5)
B) Wars and rumors of wars (Matthew 24:6)
C) Famines (Matthew 24:7)
D) Epidemics (Matthew 24:7)
E) Earthquakes (Matthew 24:7)
These are the "beginnings of birthpangs." This term is like the Braxton-Hicks contractions before the birth and perhaps the first widely spaced contractions leading up over hours (and in a few cases, days) to intense labor and birth. In recent years there have several severe earthquakes. Recent examples have been in Indonesia and Japan. However, these are but warm-ups for the terrible earthquake to come which will knock down all Gentile cities (Revelation 16:18-20). It will seem as if the earth itself wobbles (which may turn out to be literally true—see Isaiah 24:18-20). This last earthquake will be massively greater than any previous one. In today's terms a magnitude 9 earthquake would be a horror. Given the massive damage caused not only to cities but to islands and the land itself, it would be reasonable to take a rough guess at magnitude 100 for the last terrible earthquake, even considering that our scale for measuring earthquakes is logarrithmic so that each rise of a full integer means 10 times the force. No wonder that the oceans will roar as well!
F) Persecution and worldwide hatred of Christians (Matthew 24:9)
G) In reaction to that persecution (see Matthew 13 and the "stony ground" hearer of the Word), betrayal of true Christians by counterfeit brethren within congregations (Matthew 24:10-12). There will be false prophets too to add to the deception caused by false Messiahs. As in Matthew 13 the true believer is the one who from good ground bears fruit, so the believer in Matthew 24 is marked by endurance.

(For more detail, see my book Endurance: How Faith Helps You Win the Race, published by Trafford Press in 2011.) Literally, Matthew 24:12 says that the love of the majority will grow cold, just as Paul states in 2 Thessalonians 2:3 that the apostacy ("falling away" in the King James Version) must precede the return of our Lord.

H) The worldwide preaching of the Gospel (Matthew 24:14) I will bypass verses 15-20 because I believe that these verses focus primarily on the impending destruction of Jerusalem which came in 70 AD, although it is clear that the miseries of the destruction of Jerusalem under Vespasian and Titus are a miniature of the coming miseries of the worldwide destruction of civilization and the environment portrayed graphically in Revelation. For a time people will want to die but be unable to do so. Suicide will be impossible. Revelation 9:6. Matthew 24:21-22 make it clear that the judgment will be so severe that the human race would be exterminated were not the judgment cut short from its course. Perhaps making death temporarily impossible is part of God's preservation of the human race from the normal consequences of its sin. Even so, the time of Revelation witnesses a population implosion over a 7-year period, not the population explosion which concerns planners now. Then our Lord amplifies His warning against false Messiahs in verses 23-28.

I) Abnormal behavior and appearance of heavenly bodies of Creation. (Matthew 24:29)

J) The sign of the Son of Man in the heavens followed by His return to earth. (Matthew 24:30)

K) Angels performing their duties of gathering the elect from all locations in earth and heaven for the Last Judgment (Matthew 24:31, see also Mark 13:27). Notice that angels also are present in the description of the judgment in Matthew 25:31-46.

The Apostle Paul, in his last writings on earth, describes the moral conditions near the time of the end. In 1 Timothy 4:1-5, Paul again warns of the apostacy to come that he mentioned in 2 Thessalonians 2. He adds two further details: commanding to abstain from foods and forbidding to marry. Paul carried on the doctrine which Peter accepted as part of his vision to preach to the Gentiles found in Acts 10 and repeated in Acts 11. Just as all foods were now clean, so all nations were equally clean before God. Commandments to abstain from certain foods detracted from this lesson that God was teaching His apostles. As we have discussed before in 1 Corinthians 7, only those healthy adults specially equipped to live singly should voluntarily abstain from marriage, like Paul himself. Most healthy adults, like Peter and the other apostles, needed to be married for best spiritual health. Violation of these principles fosters the immorality that accompanies the end.

In 2 Timothy 3:1-5 Paul gives a list that highlights personal conduct rather than church doctrine. Judge for yourself how closely the world answers to Paul's description of the prelude to the Last Days. (I am writing this in the early summer of 2012.) The moral features of end-time humanity are described as:

A) Lovers of themselves
   Modern psychology has lost any sense of sin and most modern religion has lost any sense of self-denial. This spirit of unqualified love of self is foreign to the Lord Jesus Christ. Matthew 16:24-27 and compare Titus 1:16. The Bible does not commend self-hatred either (Ephesians 5:29) but it does require us to track down and kill remaining sin within us (Romans 8:12-16).

B) Covetous
Look at all the recent Ponzi schemes and insider trading guilty pleas as recent examples. Virtually all theft, a violation of the Seventh Commandment, has roots in covetousness, a violation of the Tenth Commandment. For the future, look at Revelation 18, especially starting with v. 9.

C) Proud
This is close to a universal sin in today's world and was considered one of the Seven Deadly Sins in the medieval world. Solomon condemned this sin repeatedly in Proverbs. Our Lord Jesus gave one antidote in John 15:5: *"without Me you can do nothing."*

D) Blasphemers
How often does one hear the names of God and of Jesus Christ used as swear words? Is this not true even in radio and television?

E) Disobedient to parents
This is so commonplace that it seems normal, even though this is like the frog being slowly simmered to death. Parental discipline has likewise broken down, perhaps in part because of long hours and in part because many parents really don't care. Divorce aggravates these problems. But our Lord Jesus predicted family division in Luke 12:52.

F) Unthankful
This is not new. When Jesus healed 10 lepers at once, only one returned to give thanks. Luke 17:12-19.

G) Unholy
The basic idea of holiness is separation from sin plus separation to the service of God. How rare this is in the modern world!

H) Without natural affection (especially towards one's family)
Where do we even begin? We have an increasing problem of both physical and sexual abuse within the family. Husbands and wives argue in terms that would make sailors blush and scald the paint off a ship. Before and during divorce, hatred is often substituted for the natural affection between husband and wife. In turn, children turn on their parents and in a few infamous cases murder them. Luke 12:52 is again terribly descriptive.

I) Truce-breakers
How many people break their word? Albert Speer of Nazi Germany, looking back in prison, gave a historical example. The Nazis decided to give Foreign Minister Ribbentrop a copy of all the treaties he negotiated. They realized in gathering them that Germany had violated almost all of them. When the copies were given, they laughed. But God will laugh at these breakers of treaties. Psalm 2:4. This warning is not limited to Nazis but applies to everyone.

J) False accusers (breakers of the Ninth Commandment)
The classic Old Testament example is Jezebel framing Naboth by false witnesses. 1 Kings 21. The Lord Jesus received similar treatment at the hands of His judges. Mark 14:55-59; Matthew 26:59-62.

K) Incontinent (if we take this almost literally, Paul is describing someone who has so little self-control that he is morally like a full-grown who requires diapers. Whenever this occurs in the physical world, it is a terrible burden. But Paul is not describing someone who is tragically helpless but someone who is morally filthy. I would understand this as the moral gutter generally.)

L) Fierce
Nazi concentration camps and Communist prisons have been sites of some of the worst atrocities in human history. Such conditions persist in North Korea. But other murderers have followed in their footsteps on a smaller scale.

M) Despisers of those that are good (compare 1 Peter 4)

N) Traitors
Judas is the greatest example, but in the apostacy to come many will behave like him. Matthew 24:10. Pray to our Lord that He will keep us faithful.

O) Heady
The basic meaning is rash or extremely imprudent.

P) High-minded
The basic idea is intellectual conceit. How much of this do we see in higher education?

Q) Lovers of pleasure more than lovers of God
Are we willing to set aside what we want to do what God wants?

R) Having [an outward] form of godliness but denying its power (i.e. the Holy Spirit)

Do we depend on our own powers or upon the Holy Spirit?

In 2 Peter 3, the central theme concerning the Last Days (v. 3) is the deliberate ignorance of past history as a warning of the coming destruction of civilization and subsequently of the world itself. The scoffers "walk in their own lusts" (how descriptive this is of modern times!) and say that everything has continued without interruption since the world began. Peter points out that these scoffers ignore Noah's Flood, as most intellectuals do today. In fact it is intellectually fashionable to deny even that the world has been created by a superior intelligence, let alone by the God of the Bible. In 2 Peter 2, Peter denounced false prophets within the Church in similar terms and in addition taught that the deliverance of Lot from Sodom is a microcosm of the deliverance of the righteous from the worldwide judgment of the whole world by fire to come. Taking the chapters in combination, it seems that Peter is giving prophecy that near the end scoffers will mock the true stories of both Noah and Lot. In addition, these scoffers mock Creation itself. Modern intellectual theory mocks the very ideas of sin and judgment. But in the end the curses in the Bible (especially the warnings of Moses in places such as Deuteronomy 4, 28 and 32 and in the Psalms of imprecation (for example Psalms 7:11-17, 9:15-17, 69:22-28, 73:17-20 and various others) and also the warnings of the Lord Jesus (for example the Sermon on the Mount when it mentions the fire and also Luke 16:19-31 and Matthew 25:31-46, among many others) will catch up to these scoffers, fasten upon the scoffers with an unbreakable grip and visit perpetual destruction and torment upon them.

Once again, in the end unbelief kills forever.

Our final verse for this study is Revelation 9:21, which lists four sins that the human race refuses to surrender in the face of the judgment of God. They are murders (for example, abortions and all sorts of true crime episodes and concentration camp deaths in numerous countries), "sorceries" (the Greek word has the flavor of drug inducement, which certainly matches the modern age of the use of many drugs to avoid one's own conscience, from alcohol to marijuana to amphetamine to opiates to bath salts, among others), fornications (all types of sexual sins which we have already discussed) and thefts. All four of these match the contemporary world uncomfortably well. The old joke about the light at the end of the tunnel actually being a freight train begins to lose its humor. In our case the light at the end of the tunnel may be the fiery wrath of God. I have no timetable, but I cannot be shocked if the final countdown to the Last Judgment starts before I have left this earth, and I am over 60 years old. When a forest is bone-dry, any forest ranger warns of extreme fire dangers. Does fire come every time? No. But that does not mean that the ranger is wrong to sound the warning. Or a doctor who observes a fatal condition cannot know the precise time that a patient may live. Jonah was right to sound his warning of destruction within 40 days to the Nineveh of his day. The people repented, and God postponed the judgment of that city for roughly 200 years. So far I see abundant indications that the world is ripe for the judgment of God with no signs of mass repentance in the modern world, and the drift is clearly to the worse with each decade. So I sound my warning without a specific schedule attached. That knowledge God has reserved for Himself. But be warned that it may be very close. I myself could have a remaining physical life span of 3 seconds or 3 decades, more or less. Our civilized world may have less than 10 years left, including the 7 years of the Great Tribulation, or it may have a century or two left as in Nineveh's case or even longer. In any case, I plead with you to repent and surrender to Jesus Christ as your Lord and your God, as Thomas the Apostle did. Only in that way can your eternity be safe and joyous.

A Christian View of Death

Death. *Todt. Mort.* In any language, it is a word that conveys finality and sometimes terror. Except in rare cases, it introduces us to mourning and sadness. The family of the deceased faces a time of wrenching change on top of mourning. Such is the wages of sin, starting with Adam and Eve and proceeding down the history of the human race.

Like all stress, death tends to lay the human heart bare. An actor relishes a death scene because it gives him or her an opportunity to showcase his or her talent. In history, courage at the scene of their deaths has brought respect to the memories of Anne Boleyn and to Marie Antoinette. Voltaire is remembered for offering half his fortune for anyone who could extend his life by 6 months. There were no takers. Luther's death was marked by a serenity that he did not have during most of his life. Jerome of Prague, a companion to Jan Hus, died singing a psalm while being burned alive. Nelson Rockefeller was literally caught with his pants down when death found him in a sexual encounter with a woman not his wife. Saddam Hussein, being justly hanged for one batch of his many murders, died reciting the Islamic article of faith. Field Marshall Rommel of Germany, who had approved the attempt to assassinate Adolf Hitler, exchanged his life for the lives of his wife and son. That son, who was spared as part of the deal, became a notable political leader in West Germany and later in unified Germany. This quick survey is enough to remind us that death comes to the rich, the poor, the famous, the unknown, the righteous, the wicked—to anyone. Death is universal among plants and animals also. This is all part of the tragic consequences of the sin of Adam and Eve.

But death does not come to all in the same way. To some it comes suddenly with no opportunity for preparation. The late President Kennedy is one such example. To others there is a substantial period of warning, as with deaths from chronic illnesses. But come it will. Therefore anyone, and especially a Christian, married or single, should reflect on death and be prepared for either sudden death or long life.

There are two men mentioned in the Old Testament that did not see death—Enoch and Elijah. They were called to God alive in anticipation of the last generation of believers who will likewise bypass physical death. As the Apostle Paul wrote, "*We shall not all sleep, but we shall all be changed in a moment, in the twinkling of an eye, at the last trumpet. For the trumpet shall sound and the dead shall be raised incorruptible, and we shall be changed.*" 1 Corinthians 15:51-52. He also told the Thessalonian believers not to sorrow for the dead like those who have no hope. "*For if we believe that Jesus died and rose again, even so them also who sleep in Jesus will He bring with Him.*

For this we say to you by the word of the Lord, that we who are alive and remain to the coming of our Lord shall not precede those who are asleep. For the Lord Himself will descend with a shout, with the voice of the archangel and with the trumpet of God and the dead in Christ shall rise first. Then we who are alive and remain shall be caught up together with them, and so shall we ever be with the Lord. Wherefore, comfort one another with these words." 1 Thessalonians 4:13-18. I do not understand this as forbidding all sorrow, but it does forbid hopeless despair when the decedent was a true believer in Jesus Christ.

A surface survey of these passages shows that the Christian view of death is quite different from that of the world, especially from the view of the secular world of the West. First, death is not final for the Christian. He or she is promised resurrection and everlasting life in the presence of Jesus Christ. Second, by implication it is clear that the death of Jesus Christ Himself was pivotal and the foundation of the promises of resurrection and everlasting life in His presence. So we must examine the death of Jesus Christ to have any understanding of the Christian faith.

At the very beginning it must be understood that Jesus Christ was unique in that He did not have the same sinful nature as the rest of us. Adam and Eve were the original progenitors of the human race. As an aside we are learning from genetic study that notwithstanding vast differences in size and appearance that human beings have very few common ancestors. This tends to confirm the Biblical testimony of one common couple and the genealogy of Noah's three sons and their wives as the ancestors of all people living today. But our faith does not rest on scientific reasoning but on the revelation of God in the Bible. He is the one with all knowledge.

Returning to Adam and Eve, it is written that when they had children that those children were in the image of Adam. By that time that image included sin and mortality. In this respect the first marriage sets the pattern for all marriages on earth between man and woman. Marriage on earth is not forever; it ends when one of the marriage partners leaves this earth and this body. Neither is any marriage perfect so as to be fit for preservation intact in heaven. While marriage was given to the human race before sin, marriage has been adapted to the reality of sin so that it is impermanent, like our present bodies. Luke 20:27-38 makes at least three truths clear:

1) There is a genuine and bodily resurrection of the dead;
2) In that resurrection our bodies are fundamentally different from those we know now and are like those of the angels already in heaven (compare 1 Corinthians 15:35-49); and
3) In that resurrection there is no marriage between male and female. In fact in the resurrection there will be no gender. Therefore marriage as we know it will cease.

Instead of marriage as we now know it we will experience an incomparably greater, more intimate and more joyful union with Jesus Christ forever in heaven. This is pictured in Revelation 19:7-9 and 21:2-5. The Apostle Paul gives us some idea of the future reality in 1 Corinthians 13:11-13, 2 Corinthians 5 and Ephesians 5:22-33. On earth we are continually learning about our mates (for those who are married—if a reader is going to remain single I would pray that their intimacy with Jesus Christ would satisfy them on earth) but we can always be surprised. We never fully know them. But in heaven as members of the Bride we will completely and in every intimate detail know Jesus Christ, the Son of God. The delights of heaven will far surpass even a blessed human marriage and every other delight that we may experience on earth. *"Eye has not seen, or ear heard, nor has entered into the heart of man the things that God has prepared for those that love Him."* 1 Corinthians 2:9, quoting Isaiah 64:4.

Unless God intervenes specially, death is universal for the human race. But Jesus Christ was not made in Adam's image because He did not have a human biological father. Luke, a doctor and fluent writer, makes that clear in Luke 1:35. The Holy Spirit is the biological Father of the Lord Jesus, and from Mary His mother He received humanity but neither sin nor mortality. Jesus Christ was capable of dying voluntarily by His own choice, but He would never have died had He not chosen to die for our sins. Our Lord Jesus stated his most directly in John 10:17-18, *"Therefore does My Father love Me, because I lay down My life that I may take it again. No man takes it from Me, but I lay it down of Myself. I have power to lay it down and I have power to take it again. This commandment I have received from My Father."* Earlier in John 5:21 He said, *"As the Father raises up the dead and brings them to life, so the Son of Man raises up and brings to life whom He will."* And again in John 5:26, *"For as the Father has life in Himself, even so has He given to the Son to have life in Himself."* When we consider Jesus Christ, we are dealing with a totally unique human being Who is a fusion (historically called the "hypostatic union") of God and of humanity apart from the sin and mortality that humanity acquired in the Fall as recorded in Genesis 3. It is this unique Son of God and Son of Man that gave His life at the Cross to the kind of death that we sinners normally suffer. Not only that, but His death on a Roman cross was particularly painful and gruesome. Added to that is that His death was ordered and inflicted by human beings infinitely inferior to Himself in every possible measure. We talk in sports of "taking one for the team." But Jesus' death dwarfs even the most heroic death in battle that might earn a Victoria Cross or a Congressional Medal of Honor. Our Lord Jesus deliberately took the entire penalty of sin for each one of His sheep. *"I am the Good Shepherd. The Good Shepherd gives His life for the sheep." John 10:11.* Or as Peter wrote, *"Who His own self bore our sins in His own body on the tree, that we, being dead to sins should live unto righteousness: by Whose stripes you were healed. For ye were as sheep going astray; but are now returned unto the Shepherd and Bishop of your souls."* 1 Peter 2:24-25.

So what did Jesus mean on the Cross at the end of His agony when He cried, *"It is finished!"?* From His immediate perspective in His pain-wracked human body, His suffering was over. He had paid the full price of sin for all of His people for all time. Further, the separation between Him and His Father was over. Note the difference between His earlier cry of the formal *"My God, My God, who have You forsaken Me?"* and His present words, *"Father, into Your hands I commit my spirit."* The change back from the formal "My God" to the intimate "Father" (such as Jesus had used in the Lord's prayer and in His prayer in Gethsemane) is important. In His last moments before physical death our Lord Jesus was reunited spiritually with God His Father. He endured that separation as the price of our sin. The restoration is one indication that the price was fully paid.

The power of death was likewise finished. As Paul said, *"The sting of death is sin, and the strength of sin is the Law. But thanks be to God, Who has given us the victory through our Lord Jesus Christ."* 1 Corinthians 15:56-57. With the full payment for sin finished, its grip over all believers in Jesus Christ is likewise broken even if we must endure physical death. Even before His death, our Lord Jesus told us, "*Do not fear them who can only kill the body but are not able to kill the soul, but rather fear Him who can kill both body and soul in hell. Yes I say, Fear Him!*" Matthew 10:28 with the tag added from Luke 12:5. The Apostle Paul also testified that he was not afraid to die and would willingly die at the hands of human government if he had committed an act worthy of execution. Acts 25:11. The fear of death brings bondage to Satan. Hebrews 2:14-15.

So Satan's kingdom is likewise finished in principle, like the Imperial Japanese Navy after the Battle of Midway. Jesus Christ has already blasted an unbridgeable gap in the defenses of Satan's kingdom, and we in spiritual warfare are given the privilege of driving though that gap and of mopping up the broken remains of Satan's kingdom. In this process over the centuries as we count time (but remember that in God's flexible time—2 Peter 3:8—our centuries are a mere blink) many Christians have been martyred in the process and others have suffered physical and even spiritual wounds in spiritual battle, but these wounds ultimately bring glory to Jesus Christ and everlasting honor to those who suffer them in faith. At the end of Daniel 2 there is the vision of a fifth kingdom—the stone made without hands—that crushes all of the previous kingdoms. That is the Kingdom of God ruled together by Father and Son.

The final destruction of the shattered remains of Satan's kingdom is surer than your next earthly breath.

Our Lord Jesus in the context of His own death told His disciples that "*Your sorrow will be turned into joy.*" John 16:20. In the early Christian church funerals were often occasions of joy that the departed was now with his or her Lord. If we suffer the death of a family member, there is real sorrow. Our Lord Jesus was Himself *"a Man of sorrows and acquainted with grief."* Isaiah 53:3. But these sorrows and griefs never overwhelmed Him even though they were so strong as to cause Him to sweat blood, and they need not overwhelm the believer either. Our Lord is our example: "*Who for the joy set before Him endured the Cross, despising the shame.*" Hebrews 12:2. On the eve of His suffering and death He encouraged His disciples, *"In this world you will have tribulation, but be of good cheer. I have overcome the world."* John 16:33. Echoing this, the Apostle Paul when facing yet another shipwreck told everyone to be of good cheer because God had promised to Paul that He would spare the lives of all on board. Acts 27:23-26. Christians experience many sorrows, but their joy in their sure hope of everlasting life predominates over their sorrow.

One reason for the predominance of joy over sorrow is that Jesus Christ Himself has control over death. *"Precious in the sight of the Lord is the death of His saints."* Psalm 116:15. More directly, we are assured by Jesus Christ in Revelation 1:17-18 that: *"I am the First and the Last, He that lives and was dead. And behold, I am alive forevermore—Amen—and have the keys of hell and of death."* Since our Lord Jesus Who died for us and loves us holds the keys, there is no rational reason for a Christian to be terrorized by death even though it may be painful. If we are not to be raptured directly from the earth, He will turn the key of death at the right time for us. With our Beloved turning the key, we are safe. Beyond this, our Lord Jesus will *"change our vile body that it may be fashioned like His glorious body." Philippians 3:21*. As Paul wrote, *"For me to live is Christ and to die is gain."* Philippians 1:21. Paul wrote Philippians while a prisoner facing a capital trial, so death by decapitation was not merely a theoretical possibility but a real one as he wrote. But through the Holy Spirit Paul was not afraid and faced physical death with fortitude and courage. We can too. In some cases we may be *"delivered out of the mouth of the lion"* (2 Timothy 4:17—compare the experience of Daniel being delivered from lions in Daniel 6 or of his 3 friends being delivered from the furnace by God in Daniel 3) or we may be delivered into the hands of our Savior. We can commit our spirits to Him just as Jesus Christ delivered His spirit to His Father (Luke 23:46) and also as Stephen prayed to Jesus to receive his spirit (Acts 7:59). *"O death, where is your sting? O grave, where is your victory?"* 1 Corinthians 15:55. *"But thanks be to God, Who gives us the victory through our Lord Jesus Christ."* 1 Corinthians 15:57.

For the Christian death is a door to everlasting joy and everlasting life in a new body. As Paul wrote, *"For me to live is Christ and to die is gain."* Philippians 1:21; read also 2 Corinthians 5:6-9. He even said that departing this life and joining Christ would be far better for him, but remaining would be better for the church in Philippi. Philippians 1:23-4. Paul's appointed time was approaching, as he wrote in his final letter to Timothy. 2 Timothy 4:6.

One may object that I am advocating too much confidence or even presumption in picturing death as a door to an eternity better than paradise for the Christian. But the Scriptures tell us that as Christians we may approach God boldly in faith. *"Let us therefore come <u>boldly</u> to the Throne of Grace, that we may obtain mercy and find help in time of need."* Hebrews 4:16. James instructs, *"But let him ask in faith, nothing wavering."* James 1:6. John tells us, *"Herein is our love made complete [from <u>Strong's Lexicon</u>; the King James uses "perfect"), that we may have <u>boldness</u> in the day of judgment."* 1 John 4:17. We need not worry or doubt; we can and should rest in the finished work of Jesus Christ.

By contrast, death for the unbeliever ushers in everlasting torment and pain. For those who do not believe in Jesus Christ, life is like walking on a floor honeycombed with trap doors. We never know when the trap of death will be sprung and we then fall forever. Jonathan Edwards in his famous sermon pictured us as repulsive spiders hanging by a single thread which is occasionally singed by the fire and which might give way at any time, dropping the spider/human into the fire to burn forever. But this terrible prospect is not for the converted Christian, who is *"kept by the power of God through faith to salvation ready to be revealed at the last time."* 1 Peter 1:5.

One more delight for the Christian connected with the coming resurrection is that God will fulfill His promise that He will take vengeance on the unrepentant wicked and especially on Satan himself, the arch-villain of all history. *"And the devil that deceived them was cast into the lake of fire and brimstone, where the beast and false prophet are, and shall be tormented day and night forever and ever."* Revelation 20:10. Justice is finally served on the Serpent who led humanity away from God in the first place. By that time we also will have been perfected and will be able to see Satan's sin and that of his followers as God sees it. Satan did not remain thankful for his position of light-bearer (Lucifer); human beings as a rule are not grateful for life, for water, for oxygen or for countless other blessings within Creation that make our lives easier. In fact, being rebellious against God, they hate His people also (John 15:18-21). Now all this will be paid back and set right, for the sake of the glory and honor of God and also for the sake of His people. Heaven cannot be heavenly if sin is present there. As creatures created in the image of God, human beings do not die permanently—they are resurrected. If their sin remains, then they are banished forever from heaven into the same lake where Satan is tormented. Revelation 20:11-15. Revelation 22:11 adds that there will be no further changes of moral nature. In fact, Satan and the rest of the wicked could not tolerate heaven with its holiness any better than they will tolerate the torments of the Lake of Fire. To worship Jesus Christ as the Son of God and to obey Him would be just too much!

Finally the Scripture of Psalm 85:10 will have its complete fulfillment: "*Mercy and truth have met together. Righteousness and peace have kissed [each other].*"

"*The last enemy to be destroyed is death." 1 Corinthians 15:26.* **Its power is broken and its complete destruction is certain. As believers protected by the Blood of Jesus Christ, we survive and thrive forever. Rejoice!**

Appendix A
A Note on Male Leadership

In his biography of Jimmy Flatley (a World War 2 naval flying hero in the Pacific) entitled Reaper Leader (Naval Institute Press, 2002), Steve Ewing contrasted two styles of leadership in a military context. One type of officer led by command and fear, and the other led by example and by persuading the subordinate that the officer was in his situation with him and that they would work together to achieve an objective. To take two examples from the Army, contrast General Eisenhower and General Patton. On the eve of D-Day, Ike fraternized with some of his paratroopers to calm them for the storm which lay before them that night. He identified with his men, including the enlisted men. General Bradley was of the same type. Can anyone visualize General Patton doing that? No, "Old Blood and Guts" was a stickler for detail and severe in his discipline. Being a stickler was not for bullying, but for training in alertness and attention to detail that would save American lives and shorten the war. Obedience and endurance were prime lessons that had to be taught, and General Patton taught them well. But no ordinary enlisted man would mistake General Patton for a buddy.

Searching the Scriptures, one finds that God our Father uses both types of leadership. *"The fear of the Lord is the beginning of wisdom."* (Proverbs 1:7, 9:10, 15:33—see also Psalm 19:9 and 33:18-19 for an introduction to the blessedness of the fear of God. Note also the centurion of Matthew 8:5-10. Even the Lord Jesus feared His Father. Hebrews 5:7. So we cannot dismiss the command-and-control aspects of God's parenting of us, even though we undoubtedly enjoy the fellowship aspects more.) With the unbelieving world, He uses mostly command-and-control because the world does not willingly obey Him. One modern example might be a bailiff's command of a prisoner. He may speak quietly, but the prisoner knows that he has no choice but to obey. Take as another example the Exodus generation, to whom God first gave the Ten Commandments. Was there any negotiation or explanation of the Ten Commandments or the reasons for them? No! They were given as categorical orders to be obeyed. God's voice was so overpowering that the people begged Moses to ask God to stop speaking because they were afraid that they would die on the spot (Exodus 20:18-20).

Even Abram (not yet renamed Abraham) was commanded to leave Ur of the Chaldees (Genesis 12:1) as an order, not as a matter for discussion or questioning. There was a promise attached because Abram was more amenable to God's leadership than was the Exodus generation, but the element of command and control remain in God's leading of Abram. As Abram progressed in his faith, we find much intimacy and discussion as the renamed Abraham prayed when God revealed to Abraham the coming destruction of Sodom and Gomorrah (Genesis 18). By this time Abraham was a friend of God (Isaiah 41:8) and the method of leadership that God used had much more of teaching and of discussion and fellowship than of strict command. Yet God's pronouncement of doom still stood notwithstanding Abraham's intercession.

Moses shows a similar progression. When he first encountered God at the burning bush in Exodus 3, he was ordered to take off his shoes and then to go back to Egypt to lead God's people Israel. His question as to the name of God was intelligent. But a considerable part of Moses' discussion at the start of Exodus 4 was a string of excuses to get out of obeying, but God would not be put off. After much experience, Moses too became a friend of God (Exodus 33:11). In John 15 our Lord Jesus indicated that His disciples were progressing from servants to friends (especially John 15:15). Returning to our military example, a raw recruit in basic training is yelled at all the time. A trained soldier may be yelled at occasionally but not as a matter of course with most commanders. With training and growing maturity comes more responsibility and a less severe approach, whether in a human military or with a spiritual soldier of God (2 Timothy 2:3-4).

God also know when to nurture and postpone either commands or teaching. For example, consider Elijah's state after the burnt offering on Mount Carmel as described in 1 Kings 19. Elijah was exhausted. Not once but twice God let Elijah sleep and also fed him. Having given Elijah strength and rest first, God then revealed Himself afresh to Elijah and gave him his final instructions.

A parallel pattern of growth can be shown in Paul's teachings on Christian maturity. Paul likens the Church as a whole to a temple built by God (2 Corinthians 6:16, Ephesians 2:21). Yet in 1 Corinthians 3, we find that we ourselves are to become builders, doing in miniature what God is doing with the entire Church. 1 Corinthians 3:5-15. Obviously this normally does not begin immediately after the new birth, although we do see occasions of effective witness by brand-new converts. Two examples are the woman at the well (John 4) and the demoniac healed in the graveyard (Luke 8:38-40). But the normal progression is salvation and conversion, then training and growth, and then greater responsibility. Titus 1 and 1 Timothy 3 show this pattern for church elders. As we grow in faith and grace, we can begin to labor with God, as an older child of a contractor may begin to labor beside his father on a construction site.

Let us transfer these principles to the family. The Scriptures say that *"the husband is the head of the wife as Christ is Head of the Church . . ."* (Ephesians 5:23) The Apostle Paul uses the term "lead" (implying companionship) to describe a relationship between husband and wife (1 Corinthians 9:5). One of the attributes of Messiah is that He will *"lead gently those who are with young."* Isaiah 40:11. Peter in the same breath instructs a wife to be obedient to her husband and a husband to honor his wife. 1 Peter 3:1-12. So the husband's headship does not justify nastiness. But the command for a wife to obey her husband does mean that even a husband-wife relationship contains an element of commanding authority on the part of a husband toward his wife, although he likewise bears the primary responsibility if he over-stresses his wife either in what he decides or in how he speaks to her. In a good marriage where both husband and wife seek to subject themselves to the Lord

Jesus, there should not be frequent need for a husband to assert his authority; in those infrequent occasions when he does so, it should be in the interest of Biblical principle and for the benefit of the family as a whole rather than to support his own mere preferences. Selfishness is incompatible with being a good mate. In exercising his responsibilities, the husband must remember in matters of preference as opposed to principle that the loving thing is to *"look upon the things of others."* Philippians 2:4.

Mary Kay Ash, the long-time leader of Mary Kay Cosmetics, as a business leader and a wife herself had a Biblical perspective on both her role as a business leader and her husband's place in her family. She called him the "Chairman of the Chairman of the Board." She was a leader in her own wide sphere of business and yet recognized her husband under God as the leader within her own home.

A wife cannot be blamed for disobedience if her husband's directions are unclear or confusing. To borrow again from military history, Napoleon's orders to his cavalry commander Grouchy at Waterloo were confusing enough that Napoleon was at fault for Grouchy's absence from Waterloo on the decisive day. A husband cannot expect his wife to read his mind, and he should remember that his wife has intelligence and permit her enough latitude to use her mind and other attributes well. Clearly, the latitude should be broadest in areas where the wife already does well and less in areas of her weakness. (If a husband for the moment thinks that his wife is stupid, just remember who chose this wife!) But nevertheless the husband should give his wife guidelines to follow. If we go back to the military analogy, she should be treated as a close and trusted executive officer and not as a recruit.

Now we should consider why God's original design calls for both a father and a mother to raise children together (although there is hope even when this cannot be done). We have already perceived that it is difficult for the same person to do well both as a drill instructor of raw recruits and as a leader of trained officers. It may be possible, but it would require a drastic change in methods which would be hard to manage. Men and women in the workplace should be judged on their own personal abilities and achievements and not by their sex. But men and women as a whole are inherently different with different abilities, even though among both men and women there is enormous psychological and physiological variation. To take one musical example, it is possible to find an adult male voice that may be able to sing at a higher pitch than a given female with a low contralto voice, but an overwhelming percentage of the time mature men sing at a lower frequency range than mature women. Most healthy men have greater lung capacity than most healthy women. Most men weigh more than most women. So most men have a greater tendency to enjoy competition, contact sports and infantry combat than most women. Most women are more adept at nurturing than most men. From my courtroom experience I have observed that women without advanced education are far better able to express themselves verbally or in writing than men of similar education. (This is one reason one observes a predominance of female secretaries and male construction workers and mechanics.) Children need both discipline and comfort, and reward and incentive as well as punishment. Our Lord Jesus knew the rewards of obedience, and that knowledge carried Him through the horror of the Cross. Hebrews 12:2, and note Hebrews 11:26 concerning Moses and reward. The parents' coordinated efforts according to the Scriptures will be more effective than either would be alone. A child will be less confused if each parent is consistently true to the gifts that God has given to each of them, even though the gifts may be very different from one another. While both parents should try to combine the two, naturally a parent will predominate toward one pole or the other. If parenting is consistent, the child can form a coherent view of each parent. But to be most effective both the comfort and the discipline must be rooted in the Bible, God's Word.

The Holy Scriptures describe God the Father, the perfect parent, as the "*God of all comfort*" (2 Corinthians 1:3) and also as a disciplinarian (Hebrews 12:4-13). So each parent should have some mix of comfort and discipline, but we will never approach the perfection of our Father in heaven. But we will get closer with the combination of mother and father than with any other structure that human beings try in a vain effort to get away from God's principles.

An essential component of masculinity is competition and growing into leadership suitable to one's God-given abilities. In military terms, one man may be capable of leading a squad where another may be suitable to lead an entire ship or even an army or a fleet. In civilian terms, one man's ceiling may be a low-level supervisor or crew leader whereas another may be able to rise to lead a large corporation. But the element of leadership is common despite the enormous differences in the size of the responsibility. One of the many flaws of our educational system is its discouragement of competition (for example, abolishing class rank) and its discouragement of boys and young men from asserting leadership appropriate to their maturity. Without at least trying to lead, a young boy cannot mature into a mentally healthy young man nor a good husband on whom his family can rely.

I am not saying that a woman should never lead regardless of circumstances. The Bible does not so teach. Deborah was a judge; Queen Esther was a tremendous leader. Huldah was a prophetess. But a woman need not be a leader to be a complete, godly woman, but a man (with rare solitary exceptions that sometimes end up being influential for centuries) must be or have been a leader in some sphere to be complete as a man, whether single or married. The Scriptures are clear that elders in the church are to be male in 1Timothy 3 and Titus 1.

Some may infer that I support discrimination against women in employment. (Note: I am not speaking of sports. At the top competitive level, sex-segregated sports competition is essential to permit woman to have any reasonable opportunity to compete. A glance at the Olympics or the world of soccer should be enough to verify this.) To the contrary, I believe that any woman who wishes to compete and gain leadership in the employment marketplace should be able to compete on equal terms on her own merits. But nobody should be given special privileges because of sex—that is unfair to other competitors. We should not imagine that equal opportunity will produce equal results in any given field of employment. Because distribution of natural ability in various fields is unequal, equal-opportunity results in most fields of employment will not be an accurate cross-section of the population as a whole but will reflect the uneven distribution of natural ability and inclination.

Equal opportunity and equal results are incompatible objectives. Insistence on equal results will result in degraded quality of economic life for all and will hinder the most gifted from pursuing a God-given calling. Each man and each woman should be able to compete to his or her ability (both as an individual and as part of a group enterprise, as may apply in a given situation) and to pursue that to which God has called him or her, within the limits of Holy Scripture.

It is interesting in this regard to observe that eminent professional women such as Anne-Marie Slaughter of Princeton University are expressing dissatisfaction with the balance of their lives after high achievement in their fields of employment. Both men and women are concerned about the balance between work and family life, but it has recently (July 2012) been career women such as Ms. Slaughter that have discussed this issue. While individuals differ, it may well be that among married people with children that women generally feel the strain of extended absence from their children either more intensely or otherwise differently from men. The historic ability of many military men to tolerate and recover from the hardship of extended separation from their families tends to support this. So does the predominance of men in long-haul trucking and in seafaring occupations. On earth extended separation from family is undesirable even if sometimes necessary. It does seem that such separation bears harder on most married women than on most married men.

But no life will be perfectly balanced on earth—we will only "have it all" in heaven with Jesus Christ. Once more we should join the last prayer of the Bible—*"Even so, come Lord Jesus."* Revelation 22:20.

Appendix B

More Questions About Selecting a Mate; An Outline of an Actual Case

As we have seen from Paul's cautious language in 1 Corinthians 7, once the Creation establishment of marriage as being between one man and one woman is honored to last for the joint lifetimes of the man and the woman, there are very few absolutes that apply to every person and every situation. The one point on which one must insist is that believers who are presently unmarried should marry only another believer of the opposite sex, if they choose to marry at all. 1 Corinthians 7:39 (applied there to widows). Another is that sex must wait for marriage—in fact a person has in God's sight already married when he or she gives his or her body to a partner (1 Corinthians 6:15-20). Serial fornication is the moral equivalent of polygamy. If one is saved while in an ongoing sexual relationship, if the other partner is willing they should marry and make it right and as permanent as any human relationship can be.

Today's culture as a whole rejects male leadership. Consider the change from "Father Knows Best" or "Swiss Family Robinson" to "Archie Bunker" to today's portrayals of either weak or sinister men. With rare historical exceptions such as "Wilberforce," modern men are portrayed as bumblers or criminals. This portrayal has a germ of contemporary realism. Men make up the vast majority of criminals (although that does not mean that the majority of men are criminals) and men are now a minority of students after high school. Even within the Christian church there is a growing trend toward female pastors, notwithstanding what 1 Timothy 3 and Titus 1 say.

In contrast to modern culture, the Bible teaches that the husband is to lead within marriage. Ephesians 5:22-24 reads, "*Wives, submit yourselves to your own husbands as unto the Lord. For the husband is head of the wife even as Christ is Head of the Church, and He is the Savior of the Body. Therefore as the Church is subject to Christ, so let the wife be [subject] to her own husband in everything.*" If one stops here, one would understand why a Christian woman who takes this seriously would fear tyranny at home. It is true that some men abuse this Scripture in tearing it away from the following verses. It is indeed true that some men have dishonored Jesus Christ by selfish use of these verses without regard to what the Holy Spirit commands them in this passage.

With male leadership and authority comes male responsibility. God has joined the two together and authority and the responsibility cannot be divorced from one another. If you look back to Genesis 3, Adam tried to duck responsibility and was given a double load of responsibility. Eve acted without reference to either God or to Adam in taking the forbidden fruit and was thereafter commanded to submit to both. With respect to men, Ephesians 5:25-29 commands husbands:

> *Husbands, love your wives, even as Christ also loved the Church, and gave Himself for it,*
> *That He might sanctify and cleanse it with the washing of water by the word,*
> *That He might present it to himself a glorious church, not having spot, or wrinkle, or any such thing; but that it should be holy and without blemish.*
> *So ought men to love their wives as their own bodies. He that loves his wife loves himself.*
> *For no man ever yet hated his own flesh; but nourishes and cherishes it, even as the Lord the Church.*

This leaves no room whatsoever for the selfish use of male authority in the home. To the contrary, that authority is to be used to build up the wife into a spiritual trophy wife, a godly blessing to the entire family. (For a more detailed description of a spiritual trophy wife, see Proverbs 31, 1 Corinthians 13 and 1 Peter 3:1-6.) 1 Peter 3:7 instructs husbands to take their wives' weaknesses into account. In this same spirit consider the implications of Isaiah 40:11 to the relationship between husband and wife and how the husband should exercise his leadership. When a husband exercises his leadership this way, a spiritual wife should find delight in following such a husband, knowing that the husband is imitating (although imperfectly) the way Jesus Christ built up and sacrificed Himself for His Church.

When the Scriptures speak of a husband sacrificing for his wife, it may indeed mean sacrificing his physical life for hers, although that is rare in the modern Western world. Jesus Christ did indeed sacrifice His physical life for each and every one of His sheep. John 10:11. More often it may mean setting aside his own preferences to attend to the legitimate needs of his wife on an ongoing basis.

There is another detail in 1 Peter 3:7 that should be noted: joint prayers of the marriage partners, who after all are "one flesh." How little this is practiced. Christians differ, but for me prayer is some of the hardest work I do. By temperament I am more inclined to read, think, act or write. At times I can settle into prayer while exercising. This is not ideal but it is better than none. Our heavenly Father is merciful. Prayer is an area in which I must wrestle even to get started. My prayer in motion also is solitary prayer, which is good but which does not meet this verse which calls for joint prayer.

"*Where two or three are gathered together in My name, there am I in the midst of them.*" Matthew 18:20. Husband and wife together qualify! But how little of this is actually done. To be sure, our busy and fast-paced lives make this difficult. Husbands, as leaders in our homes we have to move forward to regular prayer with our wives. It also means that any disputes that may obstructing our prayers must be cleared out of the way. Compare Ephesians 4:26 and for background Psalm 66:18.

The authority of a husband over a wife is not limitless as is the authority of Jesus Christ over His Church. Unlike Jesus Christ, both husbands and wives are sinners. One Biblical illustration of the limits of a husband's authority over his wife is found in the account of Nabal and Abigail, found in 1 Samuel 25. Nabal was wealthy, proud and stubborn and despised David. Nabal also had no regard for the instructions of the Law of Moses against returning runaway slaves to their masters (Deuteronomy 23:15-16). Abigail was his wife and was much wiser. Where Nabal refused any supplies to David when his men requested them, Abigail provided supplies and then waited until Nabal had slept off a binge of alcohol to discuss it with him when sober. When Abigail told him, Nabal had a heart attack and died about 10 days later. A husband has no right to command his wife to sin. His authority is bounded by the Holy Scriptures, which means real protection for his wife from arbitrary use of authority.

It is the place of a wife to encourage her husband to right behavior. In Judges 13, Samson's parents are a good illustration of a wife showing stronger faith than her husband. He rightly heeded her advice. Sarai was wrong to advise Abraham to take her handmaid Hagar as a concubine (Genesis 16) but was right in later insisting that Hagar and Ishmael leave after Ishmael had mocked Isaac (Genesis 21). Abraham as the man bore the primary responsibility for his sinful conduct and its complications, which God nevertheless used for His own purposes. Adam in the Garden tried to transfer his responsibility for partaking of the forbidden fruit to Eve, but Adam as the man was primarily responsible. So a man needs discernment to distinguish good and bad advice from his wife. If she is a godly woman and a loving wife, she will frequently be right. As in other things, a man will get better advice if he teaches her well from the Scriptures and prays with her regularly. This is an example of reaping what we sow. We cannot neglect our wives spiritually and still expect them to give us wise advice, although

God sometimes is merciful and gives our wives wisdom despite our neglect.

There is an English formula for the rights of a monarch which translates well to a marriage: the monarch and the wife have the right to be informed honestly and fully, to encourage and to warn. In no case should a husband retaliate for advice he may not like. Husbands should not lightly or selfishly disregard the advice of their wives, but do have the authority to do so if they are convinced that before God this is right and if there is no principle of Scripture to say otherwise.

Especially in modern society, men in reasonable health are tempted constantly with sexual images even if they are not seeking these images out. One finds them on billboards, in commercials for almost all kinds of television (even news, sports and business) and in the workplace. Let me assume for the moment that our hypothetical husband is not seeking out such imagery on the street or on the Internet. (If he is, that needs to stop immediately!) It would be prudent for his wife to encourage her husband to obey Proverbs 5 by drawing him to herself using her own attractions in privacy and as frequently as may fit their lives. Husbands ideally would not need this encouragement and would seek their wives out for themselves. Ideally, each act of intimacy will bind the couple closer to one another and weaken the appeal of the world's temptations. I view the Song of Solomon as portraying both the love between husband and wife and the love between Christ and the Church. Remember Paul's admonition for couples to come back together again even if there are spiritual reasons for a temporary suspension of conjugal relations (1 Corinthians 7:5). The exclusive sexual bond is a powerful adhesive helping to hold marriages together. This should be nourished.

Some men may fear the power of the hold a wife obtains with the exclusive sexual bond. There is a limit: men must remain leaders in the home under the authority of Jesus Christ. But unless used to pull men away from the Scriptures that hold of a wife is a blessing, not a curse. From Creation God designed most men to be drawn to a woman and to be held by that one woman in a sexual sense. We will not understand this fully. Proverbs 30:19. This is a powerful though secondary supplement to the Scriptures (for example, Proverbs 5) that teach men to have but one exclusive partner. It is a help on the path to holiness for a husband. If you are strongly attracted to your lawfully married mate in terms of your body, be thankful. Such a strong attraction to one another between man and woman who are spiritually free to marry each other is one (but not the sole) indicator of possible marriage. Marriage at least for believers cannot be based on physical attraction alone. But it is a strong binding factor in favor of marriage if there are other reasons that support it. Viewed from the wife's perspective, a husband's attraction to her is like strong mortar holding her home together and should be encouraged and prized. Such a relationship will also make a husband calmer and emotionally closer to his wife than he otherwise would be.

If you are a believer considering marriage and not already in a sexual relationship with someone (which means Biblically that you have already married that person, with or without the ceremony and with or without complying with legal requirements of marriage), the most vital question is whether your partner also has genuine faith in the Lord Jesus and therefore has the Holy Spirit living within him or her. Sometimes God works so quickly that a marriage seems to fall into place with a rush. I myself am still living such a blessing of prayer answered speedily.

God wants us to use our minds as well as our hearts concerning marriage. For people considering marriage for the first time, I can give some suggestions for subsidiary questions that you might consider, remembering that your intended will not get a perfect score and you won't either:

1. (For women) Can this man lead me and teach me in the Holy Scriptures?
2. (For men) Can this woman encourage me in the faith? Will she encourage me to study and to worship at home as well as at church?
3. Will my intended partner pray with me? Do we pray together already?
4. Is my intended partner lazy?
5. How much self-control does my intended partner show? (Proverbs 16:32, 19:19, 27:3)
6. What does my intended partner's speech show about him or her? Is there self-control, kindness, patience and reverence in his or her speech?
7. Does my intended partner agree that we should give regularly to a local church for the Gospel? (I think a tithe is an excellent start, although I know that some godly expositors do not believe that a tithe is required. Let's bypass that specific issue.)
8. Is my intended ever under the influence of any substance? Does he or she take any prescribed medication to influence the mind? If so, does he or she follow the prescription, and does any such medication work? Does my intended partner smoke?
9. Are you marrying this person in the expectation of "fixing" a major fault, or is this person becoming more whole and more holy through his or her relationship with God?
10. Do you agree about what church to attend and what to teach any children that God sends?

11. How much self-control does your intended show concerning finances?
12. How much time does my intended spend away from home or plan to spend away from home after our planned marriage? Different people have different tolerances here, but extended stays away from home are often a source of temptation. Are either or both expecting to spend a lot of time with the "boys" or "girls" after marriage? With some occupations periodic separations cannot be helped. If this is true in a particular case, do you believe that God is preparing you both for the strain? Can changes be made to reduce the separations?
13. We are all accountable to the Lord Jesus Christ. Yet so many people find a need to be accountable to another human being as a supplement to the primary accountability to Him. Marriage is the ultimate relationship of mutual accountability on a human level. Is our intended partner a person to whom I can be accountable on a human level? Will that person also be willing to be accountable to me?

With our fallibility, there can be only prudent advice that in some cases should be disregarded even if the advice would be right most of the time. We do not have all the answers—there are only Three that do: the Father, the risen Son of God and the Holy Spirit. Let me take an actual situation:

> A Christian man in his 40s, newly divorced for valid Biblical cause, making ends meet but not a whole lot more than that from work and rental income, with mortgages against his real estate but no other major debts
>
> Ivy League and professional education

Total separation time of almost 8 months from his ex-wife after more than 20 years of marriage
A recent weight loss of about 40 pounds secondary to the divorce
Physical examination negative for STDs 6 months after separation with general good health
One child in college full-time and one child married; both are believers
Lives in a second-floor apartment over his office
Fresh emotional wounds and sub-surface anger, especially at Satan, for the divorce

The conventional and prudent advice would be for such a man to let his emotional wounds heal before seeking another mate, assuming that he should seek one at all. One theory is that such a man is probably unable to think straight until more healing has taken place. Some men would find their ability to trust a second spouse so wounded that they may be better off seeking God for self-control (review 1 Corinthians 7:1-10). Others may find themselves in a cruel dilemma of being afraid to trust another woman and yet finding self-control almost impossible because of their built-in burning emotional and physical desire to be joined to a woman. These must seek God for direction and relief in one direction or the other.

With the same principles in mind, consider another actual case:

A Christian woman, newly widowed for less than 6 months after a marriage of over 30 years, between 55-60, and too young to claim her late husband's Social Security should she remarry
High school education

3 grown children, all married and seeking to follow the Lord Jesus
Good health and no debts
Total assets under $10,000
Works at a living wage for her son's missionary ministry; receives a very small pension from her late husband's employment
Lives in a separate wing with a separate bedroom and kitchen in a house with one of her children, his wife and 4 grandchildren

Given that she was born in the United States, her childhood was nearly as bad as could be. Some of the low-lights:

Sexually abused by one grandfather
Neither mother nor father raised her for any length of time after age 4. She was shuttled mostly among paternal relatives or people whom they selected who were willing to take her in for her labor. Until high school she did not stay in one place for as long as a year.
Her father's second wife was steeped in Old World superstition. It may well have been a blessing not to have been raised in her home.
The other grandfather, while insane, killed his wife, her grandmother. He was found not guilty by reason of insanity and confined in an asylum.
At least 20 changes in schools during her elementary and secondary education
Frequent illness, especially with repeated episodes of ear infections and foul-smelling drainage

Poorer than other students and usually unable to make routine purchases at school such as lunch milk

If we were to view this childhood profile in isolation, we would expect a deeply troubled woman who would have major trouble with any marriage she might enter and also in raising her children. Her first marriage remained intact until her husband died but lacked the emotional bonding that one would desire.

There is one important detail to add to all this. Some of her collateral relatives did have home adult Bible studies. This young girl, even if cleaning in the kitchen when the teaching was done, overheard the Word of God while staying with some of her relatives. Her life illustrates the importance of sowing spiritual seed indiscriminately. In the Parable of the Sower, God sows His seed everywhere, even on hard-packed ground that would be pavement in modern life. In this case the Word from the mouth of one of the teachers reached the young girl even though the teacher was probably not conscious that she was listening. In God's sovereign grace His Word took root in the young girl's heart that had been plowed and furrowed by hardships. This young girl was everyone's step-child on earth, but from the vantage of heaven she was God's child notwithstanding all of the horrible experiences of her childhood. But few understood this at the time, and the girl's grasp was no doubt elementary at first.

Conventional, prudent advice for her from a financial standpoint would be to remain unmarried at least until age 60 when she could then claim on her deceased husband's Social Security. Many would question whether she should remarry at all or especially whether she was ready for marriage so soon after her husband's death. As matters stand, she has her place to live near her son and his family, which is more support than many widows receive. Why risk that for a new marriage?

So far I have presented these two cases separately, as indeed they began. Most likely the consensus advice to each, whether within the Christian church or the professional secular world, would be to remain single for a substantial period of time.

{If you are using this book in a class or discussion group, you may wish to have a discussion based on the summaries of the situations of each of these people.}

To proceed on to the actual course of events, one needs to consider whether or not these two appear suitable for each other. Many advisers would be concerned that the woman was born more than a decade before the man. There is an apparent mismatch in their educational level. Neither appears strong financially, although both have avoided unsecured debts. Neither has a place where a married couple would enjoy living. From her family background, the woman appears to have a high probability to be a very troubled wife and also to have emotional difficulty with sexual relations with a man. Multiple changes, both fast and stressful, would be necessary to prepare a home if these two people decided to marry each other. Most counselors would understandably advise caution, whether in a Christian church or in the secular world.

Contrary to conventional wisdom, over 15 years ago these two people did buy a home together and marry each other within 6 weeks of having their first lunch together. The wedding stunned their community at the time. And the marriage has worked wonderfully for both from the start. Each by the grace of God has enjoyed the dimensions of love within the marriage: joint spiritual worship, broad companionship and mutual physical love. What was the difference? God Himself selected these two people for each other, just as God indicated His selection of Rebekah for Isaac by causing Rebekah to water the camels of Abraham's trusted servant in answer to that servant's prayer. (The complete story is found in Genesis 24.) "*Whoever finds a wife finds a good thing and obtains favor from the Lord.*" Proverbs 18:22. And what about the woman's terrible experiences in childhood? The Holy Spirit lives within her. He Himself had repaired the damage to her, so that she was and remains an intellectually, emotionally and spiritually healthy woman. "*Greater is He that is in you than he that is in the world.*" 1 John 4:4. The presence of the Holy Spirit made her effectively able to drive off (see 1 Peter 1:1-5, 2 Peter 1:1-4 and Ephesians 6:10-18) all the cruel attacks that Satan unleashed. Like Job, she prevailed in the end through the grace and power of God. One member of the church where they were married was overheard to say right after the marriage, "I don't know who she is but she is the best thing that ever happened to him." That's going too far; the best thing that has ever happened to any man or woman is to be transformed by the Lord Jesus Christ and to be taken from the kingdom of darkness to the Kingdom of God. But this marriage for the man was second to nothing else but that glorious life-giving event.

And what of the woman? She has flourished within the marriage. Her Bible knowledge and her Christian joy have multiplied many times during the marriage. The combination of male and female has many times the strength of these two separately. There are things yet to be corrected and improved, but they serve Christ as one team much better than they could serve Him separately. For him especially God's observation about Adam in the Garden applies, *"It is not good for man to be alone. I will make him a help suitable for him."* Genesis 2:18. For her the same has been true. It turned out that the apparent educational mismatch concealed their complementary intelligences. But their own qualities are not the reason for the success of this unconventional marriage. The reasons for that are the sovereign grace and mercy of God through our Lord Jesus Christ.

What can we learn from this unusual but true story? One thing is that we cannot always judge by appearance. As the investment disclaimers say, "Past performance is no guarantee of future results." Salmon even married a former prostitute, the Canaanitess Rahab who normally would have been accursed and would have been marked for death in Jericho. From this union came Boaz and eventually David. A troubled background is not an absolute disqualification for a marriage partner despite the risks. The Emperor Justinian found his earthly fulfillment in Theodora, an actress of questionable reputation. As long as she lived, she was a tremendous help to him. God has every right and all power to work in unusual ways. A second lesson is that there is a time for boldness as well as for prudence. Boaz was very bold in marrying Ruth, a penniless foreigner, and he was blessed for it. There are times in our lives where caution will not do, where God demands that we go forward in faith. When God gives that call, we need to heed it even if we do not yet know why and even if we are cautious by nature. So it was with Abram leaving Ur of the Chaldees and then leaving Haran after the death of his father. And so it was with Sarai following her husband wherever he went. The ultimate time to go "all in" is in trusting the promises made by the Lord Jesus Christ to forgive the sin of all who will believe and trust Him for their salvation and who in principle will commit to obey Him as Lord.

This unusual marriage is but a tiny microcosm of the blessings in store for those with Christian faith that produces Christian character and obedience to the Lord. Once again, nothing here is to the glory of the man or of the woman. All the glory goes to God the Father, Son and Spirit, Who took two pieces of clay and joined them together to produce mutual blessing.